T0345552

NAPOLEON AT PEACE

NAPOLEON
AT PEACE

How to End a Revolution

WILLIAM DOYLE

REAKTION BOOKS

For Boney's biggest fan

Published by Reaktion Books Ltd
Unit 32, Waterside
44–48 Wharf Road
London N1 7UX, UK
www.reaktionbooks.co.uk

First published 2022
Copyright © William Doyle 2022

Printed and bound in Great Britain
by TJ Books Ltd, Padstow, Cornwall

A catalogue record for this book is available from the British Library

ISBN 978 1 78914 617 2

Contents

Alexis Chataignier, 'Bonaparte, First Consul, Putting Away His Sword after the General Peace', 1802, stipple engraving.

Preface

'So long as Bonaparte was not making war, his prodigious activity
was entirely directed within. It was in peace . . . that he shone
with the purest brightness, and through his rarest qualities.'[1]

COUNT MATHIEU MOLÉ

N apoleon often said, recalled his minister of the interior,
Jean-Antoine Chaptal, 'that when he came to take
charge of the government, the French Revolution had
not come to an end'.[2] It is true that within weeks of taking power
he was declaring that it had, but it took almost three years to turn
wishful thinking into a reality, celebrated in 1802 with the Peace
of Amiens and a concordat with the Catholic Church. This book
aims to analyse how it was done.

It is not intended as a comprehensive survey of the consulate.
Some of its greatest achievements, such as financial stabilization
or the Civil Code, get little or no mention. These were establishments for the future, but this study quite deliberately does not look
forward to or discuss later achievements. It is more about round-
ing off a troubled past; laying foundations rather than erecting
superstructures. Echoing the first words of Alexis de Tocqueville's
Ancien Régime, it tries to offer not a *history of* the consulate, but a
study on the consulate, concentrating mostly on how what preceded
it set an imperative agenda for remedial action. Most of what happened in the French Revolution was neither planned nor foreseen
in 1789. But decisions taken in the course of it created intractable
problems which prolonged the revolutionary process and polarized the country. For a decade, nobody seemed capable of resolving
them, with or without violence. The main issues were religion, war

and monarchy, all three compounding endemic disorder, both within France and in its overseas empire. Napoleon's achievement was to find solutions for the three great problems, thereby diminishing much of the disorder that went with them – in metropolitan France at least. His attempted colonial solution failed but still marked the end of the Revolution in a different way. Everything came together with the peace of 1802, marking the closure of the Revolution, which had opened Napoleon's path to power. It is true that international peace lasted barely a year, and harmony with the Catholic Church not much longer, but what followed began a new phase in the history of France, posing different problems.

Each of the problematic legacies of the Revolution receives a separate chapter, culminating in a final survey of the resulting fragile peace. Inevitably this arrangement involves some repetition, hopefully kept to a minimum. An epilogue highlights the consulate's great failure – to recreate the foundations of France's flourishing pre-revolutionary Atlantic empire. Each chapter traces its subject to its origins and follows its evolution down to 1799, before analysing how the first consul confronted the problem. Wherever possible, his own earlier attitudes and involvement are identified, widening out into full discussion of how he deployed power when he achieved it.

Napoleon's posthumous fame rests largely on his military achievements. Yet between 1799 and 1805 he only fought one battle, which he nearly lost. Only his rival Jean-Victor Moreau's later victory, and political accidents in Great Britain, secured the triumphs for which he took so much credit. But Napoleon was a believer in luck, and he knew how to make the most of it.

Louis-Marie Autissier, *Admiral Sir Sidney Smith*, 1823,
watercolour on ivory.

Introduction

Napoleon's vanity knew no limits. His successes he regarded as his alone, his setbacks invariably the fault of others. In exile on St Helena after Waterloo, he spent the final six years of his life blaming his defeat, by what he called a mediocre general, on the incompetence of followers, even though these were men who had risked everything to rally to his unexpected return. The escape from Elba in March 1815 was the last flash of his legendary boldness; but boldness was at least one quality he admired in others, even his enemies.

Among the latter was Sir Sidney Smith. 'Sydney Smith', he told his doctor on St Helena, 'is a brave officer . . . He is active, intelligent, intriguing and indefatigable' – although even then he could not refrain from condemning Smith's military misjudgements and concluding that, for all his qualities, he was 'half mad' (*mezzo pazzo*).[1] Their paths had crossed twice on the battlefield. When, in 1793, at the Siege of Toulon, young Captain Bonaparte first made his military mark with the plan which drove Anglo-Spanish occupiers from France's naval fortress on the Mediterranean, he was compelled to watch as Sidney Smith set fire to the moored French fleet and destroyed fourteen warships before sailing off.[2] Then, six years later, General Bonaparte's siege of Acre, on the Syrian coast, was thwarted when a squadron under Smith's command captured a French convoy carrying siege guns and was able to keep the fortress constantly supplied from the sea.[3] Smith's ships shadowed the plague-stricken French army as it trudged back to Egypt in the summer heat. It then covered the landing of a Turkish force of 15,000 men at Aboukir, where, a year earlier, Nelson had destroyed the fleet that had brought the French to Egypt, and so marooned them there. But still they held Egypt, and, depleted though they were, they proved more than a match for the Turks. Now it was Smith's turn to watch helpless from the sea on 25 July as his allies were routed and massacred by Bonaparte's much smaller force.

Smith was in Levantine waters in two capacities. He was both commander of a naval squadron under the orders of Lord Nelson, and joint minister plenipotentiary to the Turkish sultan, reporting directly to London. This left him subject to contradictory instructions. From London he was authorized to help the sultan expel the French invaders from Egypt. The orders from Nelson were to blockade them there until they surrendered.[4] By the spring of 1799 the Directory in Paris clearly regarded Egypt as a lost cause. The invasion of this Turkish territory had set off a diplomatic chain reaction which brought together a new anti-French coalition in Europe. Russian, Austrian and British forces rapidly forced the Republic on to the defensive from Italy to the North Sea, and on 26 May an urgent order was sent to its most successful general to return from Egypt. Intercepted by the Royal Navy, the message never reached him, but by now attempting a return was much on Bonaparte's mind. He had never intended in any case to spend so long in the East, much less to be cut off there.[5] Even before the siege of Acre he had sent a secret emissary to Smith offering to evacuate Egypt subject to certain conditions.[6] After Acre, Smith could reasonably expect new overtures, and after Aboukir they came. While the Turks were sent another offer to evacuate Egypt, Smith was approached with a proposal for an exchange of prisoners. The main purpose of this contact, however, seems to have been to learn news from Europe. 'For six months', reminisced General Louis

Viesse de Marmont, who organized the approach, 'we had heard nothing ... We knew vaguely that war had begun again in Europe but we were unaware of how it had gone.'[7] Sir Sidney proved more than happy to tell them. Italy was lost to the French, he declared, well aware that the general who had made it theirs in 1797 was now trapped on the shore he was blockading. And to emphasize the point he gave the French negotiator two-month-old French-language newspapers that reported the Republic's defeats in detail. Finally he passed on the news that the British had intercepted the notice of recall sent to Bonaparte in May. He emphasized that no return was possible so long as Egypt was blockaded.

Smith's motivations and calculations are hard to decipher.[8] He certainly hoped to demoralize the French by spreading news of defeat and disaster in Europe. By this time, in fact, the military situation of the Republic was improving, but nobody in the East, Smith included, yet knew that. Nothing, meanwhile, seemed more likely to weaken the resolve of the French Army than tempting the general who had led them to the banks of the Nile to leave. And nothing was better calculated to spur his departure than news of fighting in Europe. Marmont sensed the importance to Bonaparte of 'not letting new reputations grow',[9] and noted that the moment they arrived the general locked himself away for four hours with the newspapers sent by Smith. When he emerged, it was to set in motion a plan already hatched for escaping from Egypt. Smith's bait had worked. He had hinted that his ships could not be permanently on station, and that sooner or later he would be obliged to replenish his supplies. This was enough for Bonaparte to order Honoré Joseph Antoine Ganteaume, the French admiral in Egyptian waters, to prepare the two frigates remaining under his command for sea. They were almost ready when, on 17 August, Ganteaume reported that Smith's blockading ships had disappeared. They had indeed left for Cyprus to resupply themselves – and perhaps quite deliberately in order to offer the French commander-in-chief a window of escape. At once he seized his chance. Dashing in secret to the coast with a choice handful of trusted lieutenants, he embarked on the evening of 22 August without prior notice to his chosen successor, general Jean-Baptiste Kléber. He had summoned Kléber to an 'important' meeting, but by the time the latter arrived the next day, the ships had sailed, as all on board now knew, for France.

Sir Sidney Smith had every reason to feel satisfied. Sooner or later, he knew, the demoralized Kléber would have to negotiate a withdrawal of his steadily declining force: within a month the French commander contacted the Turks proposing this. Bonaparte, meanwhile, was in peril on the sea. There were plenty of British warships, particularly in the western Mediterranean, on the lookout for French sails. At least once a whole squadron sighted his flotilla. Amazingly, it eluded them. But even if he made it to France, the situation of the Republic sounded beyond saving – although Smith's information was no more up to date than that he had revealed to the French. And if, despite everything, the fugitive general returned to a position of power in France, he might even be instrumental in restoring a Bourbon king. Everybody, on both sides of the English Channel, remembered how General George Monck had restored Charles II to the thrones of England, Scotland and Ireland in 1660. This was certainly the hope and inspiration of the royalist émigrés whose company the francophone (and Francophile) Smith enjoyed. Several of them served on his ships under assumed names.[10] Royalist agents had been quietly attempting to win Bonaparte over to their cause ever since his Italian triumphs in 1796, and he had never explicitly rebuffed them.[11]

But among all these hopes and speculations, only the removal of the French Army from Egypt came to fruition. Even that took two more tortuous years of negotiation and intermittent fighting. In the meantime, Bonaparte had been allowed to achieve his long-nurtured dream of escaping to Europe. He was full of justifications for leaving his army, as Kléber effectively put it, in the shit:[12] he had actually been recalled; he had made Egypt secure against the Turks by the victory of Aboukir; his military skills were needed to rescue the Republic from disaster. His true motives were more personal: this was his chance to grasp the supremacy in France, which had been his innermost ambition since his triumphs in Italy. 'That man', he is reputed to have said of Sidney Smith, 'made me miss my destiny.'[13] What he presumably meant was that the failure to take Acre prevented him from marching on to Constantinople and establishing a new Alexandrian empire in the East. Eastern dreams never left him; but he must have known that a more certain destiny awaited him when he escaped from Egypt. So, far from thwarting Napoleon's destiny, Sidney Smith's deliberate neglect allowed him to seize it.

Alexis Chataignier and Edme Bovinet, 'The Three Consuls in Profile
(Bonaparte, Cambacérès, Lebrun)', *c.* 1799–1804, engraving with etching.

1

Taking Control

Napoleon was never without ambition, but until he was 23 it did not run beyond his native Corsica. He grew up hero-worshipping Pasquale Paoli, who had led Corsica's struggle for independence from Genoa in the 1760s and gone into exile in England when his efforts resulted in the island's annexation to France. The young Napoleon, even while a serving French officer, dreamed of leading a renewed campaign for independence but found himself upstaged when the revolutionary authorities invited Paoli to return. Paoli in any case had distrusted the Buonapartes ever since Napoleon's father had thrown in his lot with the French. They soon fell out, and in 1793 Paolists drove Napoleon and his whole family off the island. Only then did he commit himself to building a career in France.

Yet his ambitions only grew, so he said, little by little.[1] It was not until his victories in northern Italy in 1796 that he began to see himself as superior to other men. The realization came upon him suddenly, after the Battle of Lodi (10 May 1796): 'I said to myself: I am the one who will end the Revolution.'[2] Only weeks later he was openly telling a visitor that 'what I have done so far is nothing yet. I am only at the beginning of the career laid out for me. Do you believe that it is to make the lawyers of the Directory great that I triumph in Italy? Do you believe that it is to establish a republic? ... The nation needs a leader, a leader lit up by glory, and not theories of government, phrases, and speeches from ideologues.'[3]

Months later, after winning the Italian campaign, he told the same visitor that 'I can no longer obey; I have tasted command, and I could not give it up.'

Within days of Lodi, his sixth victory in the month since his arrival in Italy, he was already blackmailing his civilian superiors in Paris. They decided that he should share command in Italy with the experienced general François Etienne Christophe Kellermann, who had secured revolutionary France's first military victory at Valmy in 1792. Napoleon threatened to resign, and the idea was dropped. From then on, he did as he liked in Italy. The Directory's strategy was to occupy Austrian possessions south of the Alps and use them to bargain with when peace negotiations began. But Napoleon made his conquests non-negotiable by transforming them into the Cisalpine sister republic. Ordered to march on Rome, instead he extorted a war indemnity and territorial concessions from the pope in the Treaty of Tolentino (February 1797), signing on his own initiative for the first time, in the name of the Republic. Then, two months later, he concluded the unauthorized preliminaries of Leoben, under which the Austrians recognized their losses both north and south of the Alps. The Directory, and upstaged generals still fighting in Germany, could scarcely repudiate terms that brought such a triumphant end to war on the continent. All that stood in the way of a final endorsement of these preliminaries were political uncertainties in France: would legislative councils more conservative in membership since the spring elections of 1797 settle for more of a compromise peace? The possibility was scotched by a purge of the councils on 18 Fructidor (4 September), carried out with military support, acting under orders from Italy. The final Peace of Campo Formio, broadly confirming the terms of Leoben, followed within weeks.

Almost from the moment when he took his first command against a foreign adversary, therefore, the young general had begun to dictate the Republic's foreign policy. Winning the war on the continent brought him enormous popularity, and when he returned to Paris after Campo Formio, advocates of every shade of political opinion jostled for his support. He neither rebuffed nor encouraged any of them, but he had already begun cautiously to reveal his political ideas to chosen listeners. Among them was Charles Maurice de Talleyrand, a blue-blooded former bishop who had espoused the early radicalism of the Revolution and prudently left the country in the wake of the overthrow of the monarchy. Returning from money making in America after the Terror, in July 1797 he was appointed foreign minister. 'If I were in power,' the young general wrote from Milan to the new minister, 'you would be rewarded as you deserve for your contributions to the Revolution.'[4] But, he said, the Revolution had destroyed a lot and constructed nothing. Nobody knew who would end it, but it would only be done if the forces of 'anarchy' were stopped from impeding the government. Two months later he lamented that nobody seemed to know what executive power was, or ought to be, despite a decade of endless babble.[5] Military intervention (by which he seemed to be implying the recent Fructidor purge which he himself had backed) was a deplorable way for a modern nation of 30 million to preserve its constitution. What was needed was a strong executive and a detached, unpolitical legislature made up of men of maturity and experience. He did not specify what age they should be: although he had conquered and reorganized northern Italy and won the war against Austria, under the constitution, he was himself still too young to hold public office. And so, whatever his own ambitions, as he told his earlier confidant, 'the pear is not yet ripe.'[6]

Yet Napoleon was very conscious that the prestige of his Italian victories might soon fade, and that a general who no longer commanded an army was without the ultimate sanction. So even before leaving Italy he was looking for new conquests to make. French annexation of the Ionian islands from the defunct Venetian Republic drew his attention to the eastern Mediterranean. Obsessed since his schooldays with the epic exploits of Alexander the Great, he now urged the Directory to seize Egypt from the crumbling Ottoman Empire.[7] The same idea had occurred independently to Talleyrand. Both men saw control of Egypt as a key to undermining British power in India. Great Britain now stood alone in fighting the power of France, and, on his return, the victor of Italy was given command of an army to invade England across the Channel. Whether because of the genuine difficulties of the operation, or because he was now dreaming of Egypt, he concluded that a direct invasion was too risky. 'The true moment to prepare ourselves for this expedition', he told the Directory in February 1798, 'is lost, perhaps forever. Would it not be better to send an expedition to the Levant to threaten the trade of India?'[8] At the same moment, Talleyrand was urging the same course, and within days the directors met to discuss it. Napoleon had a detailed plan ready, and, as the Republic's most successful general, he was the obvious man to implement it. The directors were also not unhappy to see such a restless figure out of the country. And so he was put in charge of the 'Army of the Orient' and sailed off in May with 33,000 of the choicest troops and the largest fleet the Republic had ever assembled.

* * *

HE DID NOT expect to be away long. He intended to return covered in glory. He did indeed make short work of the Mamelukes who ruled in Egypt, but almost at once he and his army found themselves marooned when Nelson destroyed the French fleet anchored in Aboukir Bay. Thereafter, for months on end, nobody in Europe knew what was happening in Egypt, and its French invaders were equally out of touch with Europe. Matters went badly in both theatres. Unprovoked French invasion of what was technically Ottoman territory triggered a diplomatic upheaval leading to a new anti-French coalition. Its forces were soon rolling back the Italian conquests of 1797 and threatening the frontiers of France itself. In search of new victories, in February 1799, Napoleon led an army north from Egypt towards the Turkish heartland but was forced into a debilitating retreat when he failed to take the fortress of Acre. By now he had heard about earlier French disasters in Europe and had received a four-month-old dispatch from the directors telling him he was on his own. Further European reverses had occurred since then, and on 26 May 1799 a desperate Directory ordered its most prestigious general to return to France. But its order only reached him via Sir Sidney Smith after he had decided to return anyway. As early as 21 June he ordered the ship in which he would escape to be readied. Meanwhile, he sought to minimize the failure of his foray into Syria. But the loss of over 5,000 soldiers and almost an entire battle fleet since his arrival could scarcely be disguised, and if he was to abandon his command he realized that it must be with something to celebrate. The opportunity came late in July, when a Turkish invasion force landed at Aboukir. In a frenzied attack on 25 June, the French killed or drowned 6,000 Turkish troops for the loss of fewer than a thousand of their own. It was, the general declared, one of the finest battles he had ever seen, and at once he sent a public letter to Paris describing his triumph.[9] It took two and a half months to arrive, but the news was all over the French press in the days before the victor reappeared on 9 October.

* * *

HE HAD LEFT his army in the lurch, and his contempt for responsible conduct continued when the French coast was sighted. Arrivals from the plague-ridden East were supposed to observe a forty-day quarantine; he landed immediately and set off north the next day. From Aix, the day after that, he sent forward his justification to the Directory.[10] Only the need to confront the Turkish seaborne invasion, he said, had kept him in Egypt once he learnt of French reverses in Europe. But as soon as victory at Aboukir had secured French power, 'I did not think I should calculate the dangers; I had to be where my presence could be most useful.'

It was no longer useful for saving the Republic on the battle-field. The emergencies of the spring and early summer were over. In Switzerland, the army commander André Masséna had stopped the advancing Russians at Zurich (25–30 September). In Holland, Guillaume Brune had repulsed an Anglo-Russian invasion force (2 October). But the unexpected reappearance of the hero of 1797, fresh from new triumphs in Egypt, was to prove extremely useful to Emmanuel Joseph Sieyès, another former priest.

Sieyès saw himself, not unjustly, as a founding father of the Revolution. In his best-selling pamphlet of 1789, *What Is the Third Estate?*, he had ringingly articulated the political aspirations that would drive its early triumphs. Its fame secured him election to the Estates-General, and he played a leading part in its self-trans-formation into the National Assembly. But after 1789 his influence faded. The memory of his early role won him election to every subsequent assembly, but few of his constitutional ideas were ever adopted.[11] He voted for the death of Louis XVI, but his proudest boast about his time in the Convention was that he had survived. He regarded the Constitution of the Year III (1795) as a missed opportunity, and, after the purge of Fructidor, a structure beyond effective reform. He had not approved of Bonaparte's Peace of Campo Formio. He thought that a general as victorious as this had given away too much. On returning from Italy, Napoleon had made special efforts to cultivate Sieyès, but suspicion of former nobles was one of the latter's guiding principles, and he kept his distance from this one. But while the general was away in Egypt, Sieyès returned at last to front-line politics. First he was posted as a high-profile ambassador to Prussia. His achievements there were limited, but, as the international horizon darkened in the spring of 1799, the absence of so fierce a republican came to be seen as almost as regrettable as that of the Republic's best-known general in Egypt. After the annual elections, the new legislative councils nominated him as a director, and he hurried back from Berlin, convinced that his moment had come. He had never hidden his contempt for the constitution, and he seems to have been determined from the moment of his election to use his office to subvert it. He knew, too, from the experience of Fructidor, that any extraordinary action would need to be backed by military force. He needed, as he later said, a 'sword', and his chosen instrument was General Barthélemy Joubert, the same age as Napoleon and a veteran of the Italian campaign of 1797. Joubert was now sent back to that theatre in the hope he would repeat the successes of his former commander. But at the Battle of Novi on 15 August, Joubert was killed, and Sieyès put his plans on hold until another 'sword' could be persuaded to back them. He was negotiating with Jean-Victor Moreau, a moderately successful general who had succeeded Joubert, when news arrived of Bonaparte's return. 'There is your man,' said Moreau. 'He will do your business better than I could.'

It seems clear that Napoleon had returned in order not so much to save the Republic as to seize power for himself. He had fretted on the voyage from Egypt that he might arrive too late. He must have been much reassured by his reception on landing. His progress to Paris was a popular triumph, with excited crowds hailing him as the saviour of the Republic at every place he passed through. It is true that the directors briefly considered whether they should punish a general who had abandoned his army without authorization; but they quickly acknowledged that this was impossible, if not positively dangerous. Instead, the day after his arrival in the capital, they gave him a ceremonial welcome at their official seat in the Luxembourg Palace. Then began three weeks of frenzied visits, consultations and intrigues as everybody sought to cultivate Bonaparte, and he on his side took the measure of who might best serve his interests. Only slowly did he and Sieyès come together. Sieyès felt that a general without an army did not accord him the respect he deserved. The general at bottom despised the director as a prating ideologue. It took considerable effort by Talleyrand (currently out of office), Napoleon's younger brother Lucien (just elected president of the lower Council of Five Hundred) and Pierre Louis Roederer, a prominent journalist and intellectual, to bring them into contact. Even then, Napoleon took his time to decide that other leading figures, notably his old patron Jean-Nicolas-Paul-François Barras, still a director, were not the collaborators he needed. Disillusionment with the existing constitution was general. Everybody expected some sort of coup. Would it be difficult?, Napoleon asked Roederer. 'What I think difficult, impossible even,' was his reply, 'is that it will not happen, for three quarters of it already has.'[12]

Nevertheless, reliable collaborators had to be found. Napoleon systematically lobbied all the leading generals in the capital to make sure they would follow his lead, or at least not obstruct it. Sieyès and his followers worked to persuade ministers, administrators and deputies of the need for constitutional change, and of its feasibility. Nobody specified at this stage what it might entail, beyond the creation of a stronger executive than the existing five directors. By early November the conspirators felt sure of a majority in the upper Council of Elders. The lower Council of Five Hundred was more problematic. There was a considerable caucus of neo-Jacobin deputies who had been pressing throughout the disasters of the previous summer for dramatic measures reminiscent of the year of the Terror. Although they had failed in September to get all normal laws suspended by a vote to declare the 'Country in Danger', before that a forced loan had been imposed on the rich, and a Law of Hostages introduced to allow the pre-emptive arrest of suspects in disturbed areas. Their continued support for these measures cast suspicion on the further intentions of the neo-Jacobins and gave some colour to the pretext that the conspirators would use to launch their coup. But none of these plans leaked out. On 6 November the councils organized a vast joint banquet in honour of General Bonaparte – but also General Moreau, whose military achievements were fewer, but who at least had never abandoned his army. The only public hint that something was afoot was the sight of Sieyès, the cerebral former priest, taking riding lessons in the Luxembourg gardens.

But the plan was now agreed, and three days later it went into action. The inspectors of the hall, who managed the business of the Council of Elders, convoked an emergency meeting of sympathetic deputies at dawn on 9 November to declare that the legislature was threatened with a popular uprising in the capital.[13] Under the constitution, the Elders were empowered to transfer the sittings of the councils from Paris to a place of safety: the drafters of 1795 had remembered how the sansculottes of the capital in preceding years had been able to intimidate the Convention. The Elders agreed without debate that the councils would reconvene the next day outside the city, in the former palace of Queen Marie Antoinette on the western heights of Saint-Cloud. And meanwhile, to maintain order in Paris, General Bonaparte was given command of the 7,000 regular troops in the area. The transfer was constitutional; the appointment of a new commander was not. That right belonged to the Directory. But simultaneously the Directory was ceasing to exist. Sieyès and his ally, Pierre Roger Ducos, resigned. Barras, by a mixture of threats and bribes, was persuaded to do the same. The two others, not party to the plot, were confined to their official seat, the Luxembourg Palace, by a military cordon under the command of Moreau. But would the Council of Five Hundred meekly accept transference to Saint-Cloud? The issue was resolved by Lucien Bonaparte, its president. The decision of the upper house, he declared, was constitutionally unquestionable, and, at once, adjourned sittings until the next day at Saint-Cloud. Meanwhile Paris was plastered with pre-prepared posters justifying the transfer.

Throughout these events Napoleon had behaved with public restraint. On receiving command of the troops, he declared to the Elders that 'the Republic was dying. You knew it, and your decree has saved it ... We want a republic founded on true liberty, on civil liberty, on national representation, and we will have it. I swear it!'[14] When Sieyès suggested arresting the more prominent neo-Jacobins, Napoleon refused. His aim was to destroy the constitution, but he hoped to do it without overt violence. Though the Directory had squandered the fruits of his earlier victories, he said on reviewing the troops now under his command, all that was needed to restore the Republic's commitment to equality, morality, civil liberty and political tolerance was 'a good administration' unriven by faction.

It is not clear, however, what the conspirators expected the councils to do at Saint-Cloud. They spent the preceding night, recalled the then justice minister, Jean-Jacques Régis de Cambacérès, 'in empty discussions which had no result'.[15] When, after hours of delay until their new meeting place was set up, the Elders reconvened, members who had not been summoned to the previous day's session spent time asking for evidence that the legislature had really been threatened by a Jacobin conspiracy. Napoleon lost patience. Striding into the hall in full uniform, he declared that the deputies were sitting on a volcano. Had not four directors (actually only three) resigned? So the Republic had no government. With internal divisions immobilizing the Five Hundred, only the Elders could save liberty and equality. 'And the constitution?' someone shouted. At this, his self-control snapped completely. 'The constitution!' he yelled. 'You have yourselves destroyed it ... It no longer has the respect of anyone.'[16] Ever since his return, he said, he had been besieged by factions seeking his help to violate it. It no longer existed, and the duty of the Elders was to put something in its place.

The troops now surrounding the palace, his patriotic 'brothers in arms', expected nothing less. And to this implicit threat he added a phrase recalled from his time striking fear into the Egyptians: 'Remember that I march alongside the God of War and the God of Fortune.' Later he admitted that these words were ill-chosen; and after he left, the deputies spent more time discussing the legitimacy of his intervention than the action he had called for.

Now he made his way to the Five Hundred. With troops visible from every window of the orangery, which was their makeshift chamber, they were well aware that they were under threat. But instead of organizing resistance, they spent hours of empty defiance in a roll-call, pledging undivided loyalty to the constitution. In the chair, Lucien Bonaparte was happy to see them wasting valuable time. Scarcely had they finished when his brother burst into the room followed by a military escort. The deputies were ready for this at least. 'Death to the tyrant!' they shouted. 'Down with the dictator!' And, more ominously, 'Outlaw him!' Everyone knew that outlawry had sealed the fate of Robespierre in 1794. They mobbed him, and he appeared to faint. His escort hurriedly dragged him out of the room as Lucien was bombarded with motions of outlawry. Rather than put them, he left the chair; but he, too, had to be rescued by soldiers. Outside, he now joined his brother, who was trying to address the troops from a frisky horse. In the front rank were the grenadiers of the conciliar guard. The Five Hundred had been infiltrated, Lucien told them, by men with stilettos, probably in English pay. In his presidential judgement, they were preventing free discussion. And as for their attempts to outlaw his brother, he drew a sword and vowed to plunge it into his heart if he ever threatened liberty. This was enough to win the soldiers over. Coming from the council's president, it even had the veneer of legality. When ordered to march in and disperse the deputies, the soldiers obeyed. The officer in charge was Joachim Murat, soon to marry Napoleon's sister. 'Citizens,' he told the deputies, 'you are dissolved.' Angry and defiant only moments before, at the sight of bayonets they filed meekly out.

So far, the legalities had been preserved, albeit narrowly. But the only legal body now left standing was the Council of Elders. Still rattled by the tone of Bonaparte's earlier intervention, on hearing what had happened in the Five Hundred, the Elders began to debate saving the Republic in their own way. Bonaparte, Sieyès and Ducos had expected to be named as an interim executive, but no such proposal was made. Once again Lucien Bonaparte intervened to save the situation. He hurriedly convened a rump of some thirty members of the Five Hundred to draft more acceptable terms. There was no prospect of bringing together the two hundred needed for a procedural quorum – although, in a foretaste of things to come, a later official report brazenly claimed that 350 were present. The meeting went ahead regardless, far into the night, and the result was a unanimously adopted resolution declaring the Directory at an end. Temporary executive power was vested in three named 'consuls': Sieyès, Ducos and Bonaparte. The councils would adjourn until February 1800, after each appointing a commission of 25, which, jointly with the consuls, would revise the constitution and draft a civil code. The resolution was at once transmitted to the Elders, where, despite a handful of objections, it was rapidly endorsed. In the small hours of the next day, the three consuls came before the rump of the Five Hundred to swear a grandiloquent oath of 'inviolable fidelity to the sovereignty of the people, the one and indivisible French Republic, equality, liberty and representative government.' The next day, they moved into the Luxembourg, the former seat of the Directory.

* * *

THE LAW HAD been thoroughly bent, and the cumbersome rules for constitutional change ignored. But the coup had been bloodless; and thanks to the general, there had been no arrests. In the decree setting up the consulate, 62 named deputies were debarred from resuming their seats when the councils should reconvene; but that never happened, and few could have thought it would. A week later, Sieyès, following his usual instincts and directorial precedents, tried to have most of them arrested and deported. Bonaparte, however, was persuaded by Cambacérès that it was enough to place them under police surveillance. Sieyès was overridden – a sure sign of where the preponderance of power now lay, and of how it would be used to reconcile rather than exacerbate political antagonisms.

Napoleon's impatience had almost turned the conspiracy into a disaster. Only his brother's presence of mind had kept it on track. Yet he was soon portraying it as a personal triumph. A proclamation issued to justify it made no mention of anyone else. He signed it alone, and in its text called himself a man above parties, the liberator of the legislature, the defender of the law, a soldier of liberty and a devoted citizen of the Republic. It was full of half-truths and downright lies about the events at Saint-Cloud, evoking the mythical daggers invented by his brother in addressing the soldiery. It was the beginning of a favourite Napoleonic mantra: that only his life stood between order and anarchy. Sieyès had carried his fellow director Ducos into the interim consulship as a faithful disciple, guaranteeing him a majority; but at their first joint meeting, Ducos was clearly in awe of the general and offered him the chair. Bonaparte accepted; but only, he said, because his name came first in the alphabet, and thereafter the chair rotated daily. Nevertheless, it was at once obvious which of the triumvirs was the dominant personality.

When a new panel of ministers was appointed (or, in several cases, reappointed), Bonaparte chose all except one. They included, as police minister, Sieyès' personal enemy, the sinister former terrorist (and, like him, former priest) Joseph Fouché. Sieyès had expected that, during this interim period, the general would mainly concern himself with military matters, while he himself would handle the civil side, including constitutional revision. But Bonaparte had views on everything. 'This man', Sieyès complained, 'knows it all and can do it all.'[17] Meanwhile he disappointed even his friends by not revealing the constitutional master plan, which they had been sure he had ready. He expressed his thoughts by gnomic pronouncements, which only exasperated his military colleague. He wanted a structure that would rest upon 'authority from above, confidence from below', but the authority which he envisaged was curiously divided. It comprised a thicket of checks and balances; even at the summit of power where all agreed the Directory's greatest weakness had been. Sieyès envisaged a classical executive of two consuls, one for foreign and one for domestic affairs, themselves appointed by an otherwise largely ceremonial head of state, the 'grand elector'. This dignitary would live in sumptuous state at Versailles with few other duties. He offered the role to the general. Bonaparte was incredulous. Such a powerless position would make him ridiculous, he said, a mere 'fatted pig'. In a bad-tempered meeting he told Sieyès, whom he was now privately scorning as the 'High Priest', that the idea was completely unacceptable. 'So', replied the other, 'you want to be king?'[18] There seems little doubt that he did, but this was another pear not yet ripe. All he wanted, the general protested, was a strong republic.

Sensing defeat, Sieyès threatened to quit public life, but Bonaparte did not yet feel he could do without the man who had orchestrated his re-entry into high politics. Flattering Sieyès' notorious vanity, he endorsed another of his ideas. The unchecked exercise of sovereign power by successive revolutionary assemblies had convinced Sieyès that any new constitution required an external watchdog to oversee its legitimate functioning. This role he assigned to a 'college of conservators' or senate of senior statesmen. The idea appealed independently to Napoleon as a way of sidelining men of distinction into grateful but impotent dignity, as he first demonstrated with Sieyès himself. He invited him to be president of the Senate and to nominate its first members. In accepting, Sieyès tacitly recognized that he would have no future share in executive power. But nor would anybody else alongside the young general. Seeing the latter's determination not to be a remote and inactive grand elector, Antoine Boulay de la Meurthe, hitherto a faithful acolyte of Sieyès' but now sensing his waning authority, began to shift his allegiance with a proposal more to Napoleon's liking. He suggested that there should not be two consuls but three, one of whom should enjoy pre-eminent executive power as first consul. Nobody doubted whom this should be, much less the man himself. He spent some days canvassing the opinion of trusted fellow 'Brumairians' as to who would make appropriate second and third consuls. He seems to have decided in advance that the second would be the minister of justice, Cambacérès, who had been the first person he visited on his return from Egypt. A former magistrate of wide experience in drafting legislation, Cambacérès had also sat in the Convention and voted Louis xvi guilty, although espousing a suspended death sentence. He was thus an authentic, and moderately republican, son of the Revolution. He would be one of Napoleon's most trusted partners throughout his career.[19] But now the first consul designate was looking for an administrator to balance this lawyer. He also wanted somebody with a more conservative record. After consultation with Cambacérès and other close confidants, such as Roederer, he settled on Charles-François Lebrun, a much older man who had made his name in the 1770s as secretary to Louis xv's last authoritarian chancellor, Maupeou. Napoleon appreciated these credentials, but also the reputation for financial expertise which Lebrun had established as a deputy during the Constituent Assembly. It was agreed that, prior to the promulgation of the new constitution, the legislative commissioners should hold a formal public vote on appointing the new consuls. But Napoleon chose this occasion for a final act of flattery, and also perhaps humiliation, towards Sieyès. Rather than count votes, he suggested that his outgoing colleague in the interim consulate should nominate the new executive. Sieyès knew what he had to do, and the commissioners endorsed his choice of Bonaparte, Cambacérès and Lebrun unanimously.

Yet apart from the supreme authority, the new constitution, which emerged after a mere five weeks of discussion, was broadly based on the ideas of Sieyès. 'Confidence from below' was enshrined in a pyramid of 'lists of confidence'. At the lowest level all male citizens were empowered to vote for a tenth of their number whom they considered 'most appropriate for conducting public affairs'. From these, the government would choose local officials, and the whole body of the list would go on to designate a tenth of their own number as a departmental list eligible for higher responsibilities. They in turn would produce a final national list, again 10 per cent of themselves, as candidates for the highest offices, including seats in a two-chamber legislature, nominated not elected. A hundred-member lower house, the Tribunate, was empowered to discuss and comment upon draft bills. Its conclusions would then be reported to an upper Legislative Body of three hundred, whose sole function was to accept or reject the proposals. But neither chamber had the right to generate bills. The source of all proposed legislation was to be the Council of State, all of whose members were directly appointed by the first consul. Here would be the real centre of power under the new regime. Asking Roederer what position he would like, Napoleon warned him not to think of the Senate: 'It's a tomb; good for men whose career is over, or who want to write books ... but you, with your talents and activity ... the Council of State is better for you. Its functions are important. You understand public affairs, you speak well, you can stand up to the Tribunate.'[20] Accordingly, when Sieyès offered Roederer the Senate, he declined. Instead he was among the first 29 councillors of state nominated ten days after the new constitution was promulgated on 15 December 1799. The council was divided into five sections, and Roederer would chair the section for internal affairs until September 1802.

The first consul designate oversaw every detail of the new constitution. It was short, terse and, unlike those of 1789, 1793 or 1795, not preceded by a declaration of rights. All effective power was concentrated in the hands of the first consul, constrained only by a ten-year term limit. 'What is there in the constitution?' ran a much-repeated joke. 'There is Bonaparte.' It claimed, however, to be 'based on the true principles of representative government and on the sacred rights of property, equality and liberty' with which the Revolution had begun.[21] It marked, said the proclamation announcing it, the completion of the Revolution's work. And although, like the constitutions of 1793 and 1795, it was submitted for approval to a national referendum, it came into force within days. The first consul asked Roederer to draft a further proclamation to inaugurate the new regime, but he did not like its first wording. 'You make me promise things,' he said, 'and I want to promise nothing, because I am not certain to last.'[22] Moreover, 'you make me promise things for very soon, and there are many things for which my ten years will scarcely be enough.' All he was willing to promise in the end was to try to 'make the Republic beloved by its citizens, respected by foreigners [and] formidable to its enemies', and to be judged by how far he had succeeded.[23]

* * *

HE WAS RIGHT to be cautious. Although, by a mixture of audacity and luck, he had managed to capture the machinery of supreme power, he knew that it was simply not enough to proclaim from that position (as he did) that the Revolution was over. Unworkable constitutions were perhaps the least of the problems that the Revolution had thrown up, and the new one was no more likely to succeed unless it brought solutions to more intractable legacies. He often said, recalled his later interior minister, Jean-Antoine Chaptal, 'that when he came to take the helm of government, the French Revolution had not come to an end'.[24]

Begun ten years earlier with such high hopes of national regeneration, the Revolution had soon polarized the entire country. Its reforms brought losses both material and mental to every vested interest of pre-revolutionary times and resulted in widespread and persistent disorder throughout the country and its overseas colonies. Irreconcilable enemies were created by the insistence of successive revolutionary authorities and their supporters on treating any opposition as disloyalty verging on treason. This mindset was evident in 1789 itself, but took practical form the next year with the first imposition of an oath of loyalty. All members of the clergy were required, on pain of deprivation, to pledge commitment to the new constitution. Because the constitution, not yet finalized, was expected to include radical Church reforms, which the pope had not accepted, there was a massive refusal of the oath. Only just over half the clergy swore it, and it split the entire nation. Revolutionary France found itself in increasingly open conflict with the Catholic Church. Contemplating the scale of its losses, the Church of Rome remained unreconciled to the Revolution and paid the ultimate price when, in 1798, French troops occupied Rome, dissolved the papal state and declared an anti-clerical Roman Republic. Pope Pius VI was arrested and transported to France. He died there. There was no pope in existence when the consulate was established, and it seemed possible that there might never be another. Yet, whatever happened, the religious question could not be ignored. So long as the Catholic Church was its enemy, the Republic could not depend on the loyalty of most of its citizens, who had been born and educated in the Catholic faith. The quarrel with the Church was the deepest national wound inflicted by the Revolution; and it served to keep open another, scarcely less profound – the issue of monarchy.

When Louis XVI turned his back on the Revolution in the Flight to Varennes in June 1791, the final spur to his departure was a crisis of conscience over the religious question. But the flight unleashed a hitherto muted republican movement and doomed in advance any hope for the stable constitutional monarchy planned by the Constituent Assembly. The king's subsequent refusal to sanction further punitive legislation against unsworn priests played its part in the build-up to the overthrow of his throne in 1792. Effected by a popular uprising in the capital, the storming of the Tuileries Palace on 10 August was witnessed by a disgusted young Napoleon. And when the deposed Louis XVI was put on trial, and then executed in January 1793, the antagonism between royalists and republicans became unbridgeable, as those deputies who voted for his death fully intended. Given the last rites on the scaffold, he was seen to die a martyr for the Catholic faith. So it was no surprise that, when rural rebellion against the Republic broke out in the Vendée a few weeks later, the peasant insurgents claimed to be fighting for both Church and King. Royalist rebellion in western departments, flaunting the sign of the cross, was never fully stamped out. It was flaring up again at the very moment when Napoleon arrived back from Egypt.

Despair at the absence of a firm, stable and legitimate supreme executive authority had set in early, as the first two years of the Republic were marked by defiance and disorder only curbed by the ruthless bloodshed of terror. All previous political writers had argued that republics could only succeed in very small communities. Experience now suggested they were right. And so, after the Terror ended, the allure of monarchy revived. But when, on the death of his sickly child nephew in republican captivity in 1795, the brother of Louis XVI became his legitimate heir, he proclaimed from Verona that in the event of a monarchical restoration he would reverse the entire work of the Revolution. For revolutionaries of whatever stripe, this meant that restoring the Bourbons was not now an option. Louis xviii's intransigence, on the other hand, positively reinvigorated counter-revolutionaries, and they never accepted the legitimacy of the new directorial constitution fashioned by the Convention. Throughout its life, the Directory was in a constant struggle to repel royalist subversion, conducted either through the electoral process or through outright rebellion. And, as the military triumphs of the mid-1790s melted into the disasters of 1798 and 1799, the chances of a Bourbon restoration by foreign armies seemed to grow. It was fear that the Republic might not survive without a stronger central authority that lay behind the determination of Sieyès and his supporters to make an end of the Constitution of 1795. But when, as long predicted by the Revolution's critics, a general emerged from the Brumaire coup as France's supreme power broker, royalists were paradoxically encouraged. Would Bonaparte use his power to restore the legitimate king, as General Monck had in England more than a century earlier in 1660?

The possibility was in every mind, including Napoleon's. In February 1800 Louis xviii himself wrote the first consul a letter to suggest it. Surely, he asked, 'the victor of Lodi, of Castiglione of Arcola, the conqueror of Italy and of Egypt' could not prefer 'vain celebrity' to true glory? 'We can bring peace to France, I say we, because I need Bonaparte for that and he could not do it without me. General, Europe is watching you, glory awaits you, and I cannot wait to give peace back to my people.'[25] Napoleon later confessed to being flattered, but he made no reply for six months.[26] He believed himself perfectly capable of bringing peace to the nation without Bourbon interference, but he needed time and some visible achievements in power to make clear that he had seized it for himself and for nobody else. And so he waited, before politely but firmly rejecting the pretender's proposal, until he could begin to close up the third great wound opened by the Revolution, the one that more than any other had turned dissent into treason:

the war against Europe. And all his previous military and diplomatic experience had taught him that the only peace worth having was peace with victory.

Alexis Chataignier, 'General Moreau on Horseback',
early 19th century, stipple engraving.

2

Winning the War

Lieutenant Napoleone Buonaparte was probably on the sea between Corsica and France when, on 20 April 1792, the Legislative Assembly declared war against the king of Hungary and Bohemia. The young officer seems to have given little thought to international tensions. His passion was the internal politics of his native island and he was travelling to Paris to defend himself against accusations of fomenting popular violence in Ajaccio. Nor did he show much interest in the war during that summer, even though it was proving catastrophic for French arms. So, far from blaming him for his part in exacerbating the troubled affairs of Corsica, the war ministry promoted him to captain and awarded him back-pay for a period when he had been wrongly thought to have abandoned his regiment. He spurned their faith in him in October by not rejoining the colours but sailing back to Corsica, ostensibly to escort his sister Elisa home from boarding school but actually to continue promoting the local ambitions of his family. Yet it was here that he had his first taste of conflict with foreign enemies. By the time the new captain arrived home, the French were at war with not only the leading monarchs of Germany but the king of Sardinia. They rapidly overran many of his Alpine dominions (the source of his power though not his title) but the proximity of his island kingdom offered the French patriots of Corsica a tempting way to prove their zeal. An expedition was organized to take the offshore island of La Maddalena, and Buonaparte was put in charge of the artillery. It was a debacle.

He was lucky not to be left stranded with his spiked guns. But the luck in which he always placed so much faith was only just beginning.

* * *

NOBODY DREAMED OF war when the French Revolution began. It is true that one of the many dissatisfactions with absolute monarchy which had helped to bring it down was the king's inability in 1787 to defend French interests in Holland, but in the euphoria of 1789 little thought was given to the Revolution's external ramifications. There was also widespread mistrust of the armed forces, or at least their officers. Accordingly, patriots were largely indifferent to the collapse in military discipline that accompanied the early reforms. The volunteer National Guard was now the preferred instrument of legitimate force. And although the French were convinced that their revolutionary example was certain to be followed sooner or later elsewhere in Europe, they had no thought of exporting the Revolution by force. Meanwhile the other powers were quite happy to see France sink into diplomatic impotence. Kings might worry about the unfortunate example of a hitherto absolute monarch systematically stripped of his powers by unruly subjects, but they showed no interest in intervening to help Louis XVI restore his lost authority. Their low estimate of revolutionary France's diplomatic consequence was confirmed when the Constituent Assembly debated the issue of foreign policy in May 1790. The occasion was a Spanish request for diplomatic – if not stronger – backing in a dispute with Great Britain over rival claims to Nootka Sound, on the west coast of North America. The Spaniards were invoking the long-standing 'Family Pact' in which the two Bourbon kingdoms promised each other mutual support. The assembly, however, declared that dynastic bonds were no proper basis for a sovereign nation's foreign policy. It declared that all treaties were subject to the ratification of the legislature. And, most grandiloquently, it proclaimed that 'The French Nation renounces the undertaking of any war with a view to making conquests, and ... it will never use its power against the liberty of any other people.' It reserved the right to defend itself if attacked, but observers scarcely found this a realistic proviso given the chaotic state of the French armed forces. The Spanish request was rejected. The new France appeared to have opted out of international affairs.

It was only a year later, when Louis xvi attempted to escape from Paris, apparently seeking the help of foreign monarchs, that the latter began to reflect on whether leaving France to stew in self-imposed impotence was the wisest policy. Now they began to utter threats. In the Declaration of Pillnitz of August 1791 the Holy Roman Emperor and the king of Prussia proclaimed the fate of the French king a matter of common concern to all rulers. Moreover, the declaration was issued in open consultation with Louis xvi's two brothers, themselves at the head of swelling and increasingly noisy bands of counter-revolutionary émigrés arming and drilling across the Rhine on the territories of German prince-bishops. In reality, the king's brothers were disappointed by the terms of the declaration, and Emperor Leopold ii when he signed it had no serious intention or expectation of intervening in France. But the Legislative Assembly convened when news of the declaration was still fresh, and paranoia haunted the delegates right from the start. Within weeks, calls began to be heard for military action against the German prelates harbouring the émigrés. The objective of this sabre-rattling was as much domestic as international. The aim was to force the king, whose trustworthiness had been besmirched forever by his failed attempt to abandon the Revolution, to reveal his true attitude to the new constitutional order. When he vetoed domestic sanctions against émigrés, the conclusion seemed obvious. Yet the king, too, had no rooted objection to war. Convinced, like the monarchs of Germany, that the French Army was in no state to confront well-drilled opponents, he saw swift rescue by effortlessly victorious foreigners as his best hope. And although the Rhenish archbishops deferred to French threats and ordered the émigrés out of their territories, this was not before the emperor had declared that he would support these imperial vassals if they were attacked. He began to assemble troops along the French frontiers. These threats were much more explicit than those made at Pillnitz; and although Leopold II still hoped to avoid war, he died suddenly as tensions rose, to be succeeded by Francis, his much less cautious son. And the effect of Austrian threats in France was to release two generations of accumulated resentment at the humiliations attributed to the alliance made with Austria in 1756 and cemented by the marriage of the arch-duchess Marie Antoinette to the then heir to the French throne in 1770. Now seemed the moment to repudiate this disastrous pact and restore French honour. Thus by March 1792 there was wide-spread agreement in political circles that war against Austria was not only inevitable, but positively desirable. The king, when he came to the Legislative Assembly on 20 April to request a decla-ration of war, was warmly received, and his request scarcely challenged. It was claimed, in accordance with the declaration of May 1790, that France was acting in self-defence, but the Austrians were secretly pleased not to appear the aggressors. The Prussians, too, though always more eager for war than the Austrians, were happy to portray themselves as standing alongside an ally unjustly attacked. The French could scarcely believe that such deep-dyed antagonists could really co-operate. They even thought the Prussians might join them. But the old German enemies had pledged mutual support in February, and Prussian troop move-ments finally disabused French optimism. France proceeded to declare war on Prussia on 6 July.

* * *

THUS BEGAN THE wars of the French Revolution. They were still going on when General Bonaparte seized power seven years later. Nobody in the spring of 1792 expected such a long, drawn-out conflict. The German powers, and even more the émigrés urging them on, thought it would be a swift military promenade, with French armies collapsing before their advance, and the populace rising up to welcome the return of the old authorities. The French legislators who declared war thought the revolutionary fervour of citizens would rout the servile conscripts of despotism, and oppressed subjects, longing to share the benefits of French freedom, would greet them as liberators. None of them was right. Almost alone among prominent public figures, Maximilien Robespierre warned of the dangers and uncertainties of undertaking a war for which no serious preparations had been made. Even if the French triumphed, he warned, their enemies' subjects would not necessarily welcome armed missionaries. And French victory would confront the nation with dangers perhaps greater than those of defeat: the historical examples of Caesar and Cromwell showed how easily a successful general might overthrow the civil power. The military adventurer whom Robespierre had in mind was probably Lafayette, the former commander of the National Guard, known for his disquiet about the Revolution's drift, yet almost certain to be given a command (as he was) if war materialized. But Lafayette was never to win a battle, or the personal loyalty of his troops. Within months of taking up his command he would desert to the enemy. He would only be rescued after five years of captivity by a more successful commander, and it was this one who would later realize Robespierre's nightmare.

Meanwhile his warnings of war's unpredictability were amply borne out. The first few months were disastrous. French troops broke and fled at their first contact with the Austrians, lynching their general. In August, France was invaded. Lafayette deserted and several fortresses fell to the Prussians. The main results of these early calamities were domestic. The true aims of those who had clamoured most loudly for war were rapidly achieved: the king did not cease to equivocate, and threats by the enemy to destroy Paris if he and his family were harmed seemed to confirm suspicions of his treason. Less than four months after war broke out, the monarchy was overthrown, amid scenes of slaughter not witnessed in Paris since the sixteenth century. Captain Bonaparte watched them from a safe distance, the first time he ever saw such carnage. He was appalled by the savagery of 'the vilest rabble'.[1] Worse was to come a few weeks later, as a seemingly unstoppable enemy advanced. Fearing mass breakouts from makeshift prisons which were overcrowded with suspected traitors, bands of vigilantes forced their way inside and butchered hundreds of unarmed inmates. Until the summer of 1792, although intermittently chaotic, the French Revolution had been relatively bloodless. The storming of the Tuileries Palace on 10 August and the September massacres, which marked the transition from monarchy to republic, changed its reputation for ever. The first French Republic was born in military defeat and domestic bloodshed. As has often been said, war revolutionized the Revolution.

For a few brief months, it is true, the situation improved. On the very day that a newly elected Convention assembled to endow France with a republican constitution, the invading Prussians were repulsed at Valmy. They beat a miserable retreat, and within weeks French armies were pouring across the Rhine, into Alpine Savoy and, most spectacularly, into the Austrian Netherlands. The predictable result was to expand the number of France's enemies. For the Dutch, the southern Netherlands had always been a vital buffer protecting them from France. For the British, who as recently as the spring had been expecting to enjoy years of peace, in isolation from continental conflicts, French occupation of the Flemish shoreline was equally unacceptable. So by the time Louis XVI was executed in January 1793, war with the two maritime powers had become inevitable. It was the French who declared it on 1 February. Just over a month later they declared war on Spain as well. Military success seemed to have vindicated the confidence that had propelled the revolutionaries into war the previous spring. Their war aims were now limitless. Jacques Pierre Brissot, the war's leading advocate, declared that France must set all Europe aflame. The Republic offered 'fraternity and help' to all peoples seeking to 'recover their liberty'. It proclaimed war against kings and aristocrats everywhere and protection for their groaning subjects – although they were expected to pay for their own liberation. And, in striking contrast to the renunciation of wars of conquest of 1790, leading orators in the Convention began to speak of annexing territories within self-evident 'natural' frontiers along the Alps, the Pyrenees and, most contentious of all, the Rhine. That meant much of the Rhineland, the whole of the Austrian Netherlands and the southernmost part of the Dutch Republic. The idea that France should aspire to natural frontiers was not new, but establishing them unilaterally, by outright conquest, was to challenge all the established norms of relations between states, just as the execution of the king threw down a gauntlet to monarchs everywhere. The revolutionaries seemed bent on revolutionizing the whole of Europe in their own image.

Yet these hopes and ambitions evaporated almost as quickly as they had arisen. For much of 1793 the Republic found itself fighting for survival. Its armies were driven out of the Netherlands and the general who had led them there from Valmy, Charles François Dumouriez, defected, like Lafayette, to the Austrians. The army which had overrun the Rhineland surrendered and returned home in disgrace. It was redeployed to domestic duties, for by then there was widespread internal rebellion. Attempts to reinforce the armies from reluctant civilians had provoked a counter-revolutionary uprising in the Vendée and guerrilla outbreaks in Brittany. Provincial disgust at the Convention's subservience to the murderous sansculottes of Paris resulted in the 'federalist' revolt in which the leading cities of the south – Lyon, Marseille, Bordeaux – challenged the Republic's legitimacy. Corsica, too, French for only 25 years, now turned its back on the increasing radicalism emanating from Paris. Notorious for their French loyalties, the Buonapartes were driven out of their native island, and the whole family arrived on the mainland with little but Napoleon's military pay to sustain them. But there, flaunting his martyrdom to counter-revolutionary persecution, he soon found employment, and was put in charge of artillery at the siege of the last bastion of domestic rebellion, the great naval port of Toulon.

The fall of Toulon to an Anglo-Spanish fleet on 29 August 1793 was the low point of the entire war for French military fortunes. The base of one of the Republic's two battle fleets was surrendered to the great naval enemy by a city in the hands of counter-revolutionaries. When the news reached Paris, it galvanized the Convention into endorsing popular demands for government by terror. The apparatus of emergency government through terror had in fact been steadily assembled piecemeal over the months since the military downturn of the spring. Every setback at the front or provincial act of defiance provoked new draconian measures designed to punish or deter treason. The link between war and terror was made explicit when, on 10 October, the Convention decreed that the government of the Republic would be 'revolutionary until the peace'. Constitutional life was postponed indefinitely in the interests of swift and savage action against anyone suspected of impeding the war effort. And yet, by then the tide was already turning. The betrayal of Toulon was an act of desperation by refugees fleeing from the reprisals of a republican army that had retaken Marseille. Bordeaux and Lyon were also recovered, and the Catholic and Royal Army of the Vendée was harried to destruction. Enemy incursions were also rolled back along all frontiers, and on 19 December, Toulon was recaptured, largely thanks to the initiative of the young Corsican artillery officer. It brought him his first and only serious war wound but also lightning promotion to general rank.

'We are killing everything that moves,' reported the Convention's representative on mission in the days that followed.[2] This time Bonaparte was not a mere spectator as hundreds of presumed rebels or traitors were shot. Most of the recorded victims of the Terror throughout the Republic were of this sort, rounded up in the centres of provincial rebellion when the Convention's forces recovered control. Though not as obviously traitors as those who had invited the British into Toulon, their defiance could only have given aid and comfort to the enemy in time of war. Accordingly, of the Terror's more than 16,000 official victims, the vast majority were condemned in disturbed areas as rebels against legitimate authority. Many died there. Terror was a reflex of emergency, a reaction to war going badly; and when the military situation was seen to improve, its necessity began to be questioned. The decision to transfer most political cases to Paris in early May 1794 was an attempt to rein in terror; but it had the effect of accelerating the number of high-profile executions in the capital just as the armies began to move from dogged defence to victorious advance. They came to an end only a month after the Battle of Fleurus (26 June) signalled a renewed French push into the Austrian Netherlands. But fear of a return to terror haunted the entire later history of the Republic; and when it seemed to be collapsing in the face of a new coalition of hostile powers in 1799, the terrorist reflex looked poised to reappear. Only a victorious peace seemed likely to banish these fears.

Lasting victory could only be assured, however, by effective organization. The outbreak of war found the armies scarcely prepared. Fears of war after the Flight to Varennes had produced some patriotic volunteering, but it was counterbalanced by a massive loss of officers appalled at the treatment of the king. Terms for volunteers were generous, including short service, and more came forward after war broke out. Valmy was won by an improbable blend of long-serving gunners and enthusiastic new recruits. Many of the latter, however, felt entitled to go home after the victories of that autumn. By the spring of 1793 the complement of the armies had almost halved. It was decided to amalgamate volunteer and regular regiments and to raise 300,000 new recruits. In many ways the first momentous step backfired. It only raised half its target number, and it triggered the most serious of all counter-revolutionary revolts in the Vendée, which eventually took more troops to control than the decree raised. But the principle of mandatory enrolment was established, and when disasters accumulated over the summer, it was expanded into the *levée en masse*, requisitioning every national resource to ensure the Republic's survival. All unmarried men between 18 and 25 were made liable to serve. The hope was to raise over half a million, and this time at least, backed by all the coercive apparatus of terror, 300,000 were certainly drafted. By the middle of 1794 the Republic had almost 800,000 men under arms, twice as many as France had ever raised before and far more than any enemy state. And they saw plenty of action, increasingly successful, which made the crumbling military morale of the Revolution's early years a thing of the past. Nobody had trusted the army then. It had imperilled the Revolution's survival. Now it guaranteed it, not only against hostile foreigners, but internally, as campaigns against federalist cities and Vendean rebels proved. By 1795 regular troops were even being used, for the first time since the twilight of absolute monarchy, to impose order on Paris. The perpetrators of the uprising of Prairial, the last popular attempt to coerce the Convention in May, were rounded up by soldiers. And when, in the first few days of October, in the uprising of Vendémiaire, a last-ditch attempt was made by royalists to prevent members of the Convention from keeping control of a new constitution about to come into force, the insurgents were mown down by military cannon fire. The officer in charge, appointed through the influence of the deputy Barras, who had noticed him at the Siege of Toulon two years earlier, was Brigadier-General Bonaparte. He could now claim for the first time to have saved the Republic from itself.

Only a few weeks earlier he had been unemployed, having refused a posting to the Vendée. The Republic's need for generals had been much diminished by a year of victories. After Fleurus, French armies once again overran the Austrian Netherlands. And when the Rhine froze in one of the coldest winters of the century, they crossed into the heartland of the Dutch Republic. The whole of the north German plain now lay open to them, and at this prospect the Prussians decided to make peace. They were in any case far more interested in securing a grip on Poland. The Dutch, now without effective allies, simply surrendered and consented to be paying French satellites. Both these former enemies now recognized the reality (if not the legitimacy) of France's Rhine frontier, and a brief French incursion into Spain soon brought peace along the Pyrenees, too. Only the Alpine frontier remained contested by the Sardinians, Austria's last significant continental ally. All British attempts, meanwhile, to establish bridgeheads on the mainland had failed ignominiously. The new government of the Directory now felt free to concentrate its resources against the original enemy in Vienna.

But the Austrians were stubborn. Attempts to defeat them on the eastern side of the Rhine made little progress over the winter of 1795–6. A big push was planned for the next spring, but after initial success, two French armies failed to join up and were driven back to the Rhine. A diversionary front was now planned in northern Italy. After some politicking, a much smaller army than those sent into Germany was placed under the command of the Italian-speaking General Buonaparte. He had been touting plans for an Italian campaign ever since 1793. Not many people thought this notoriously political general, who had never commanded an army in the field before, likely to succeed. But in the event it only took him ten days to knock the Sardinians out of the war, and he was soon engaging the Austrians on the plains of Lombardy. Within weeks he had occupied Milan, and over the next eleven months he defeated every army sent against him. The capture of Mantua in February 1797, besieged for eight months, gave him complete control of northern Italy. While French forces in Germany remained bogged down, or even forced into retreat, Bonaparte (now dropping the Italianate spelling of his name) pursued the enemy up the Alpine passes into Austria. With Vienna almost in his sight, the Austrians felt obliged to make peace. Preliminaries were signed at Leoben on 18 April 1797, almost exactly a year after the general's first victory in the field.

Bonaparte had won the war – or thought he had. Watching the collapse of Austria, even the British were putting out peace feelers. Even their usual command of the sea had been thrown into doubt when, in December 1796, a French expedition under General Lazare Hoche reached Ireland, aborted only by bad weather. In the spring, naval mutinies and a run on the Bank of England increased British anxiety for peace, and it was encouraged in April by the results of the first open election in France to the directorial legislative councils. Most of the remaining members of the Convention were defeated, and there was an influx of conservatives and crypto-royalists. British war aims had always included the hope of restoring monarchy in France, and the emergence of the new legislative majority suggested that this might be achieved peacefully. It also encouraged the Austrians to delay final acceptance of the preliminaries of Leoben. News of a victorious peace brought an outburst of celebration in war-weary France; but the terms that Bonaparte had imposed on the emperor scarcely promised a lasting settlement. The Austrian monarch was forced to give up his hereditary dominions in the southern Netherlands and Lombardy. He was to be compensated with most of the territory of the Republic of Venice, conveniently provoked into a hopeless war by Bonaparte even as the preliminaries were being negotiated. The Directory would have preferred to hand back Lombardy in exchange for Francis II recognizing France's Rhine frontier, but that was an affair for the Holy Roman Empire, not Austria alone, and it was left to be settled later. These terms, then, were not those of the French government, but rather the result of what a British diplomat called Bonaparte's 'wild and gigantic plans in Italy'.[3]

The spectacular success of his campaign there had transformed his own life and outlook. At Lodi, one of the first battles of 1796, he later reminisced, 'The idea came to me that I might well, after all, become a decisive actor on our political scene. Then was born the first spark of high ambition.'[4] Battlefield success had given him effective political independence, and in ignoring instructions from Paris he began to dictate the policy of the Republic. Ordered to march on Rome in 1797, instead he concluded the Treaty of Tolentino with the pope, turning northernmost papal territories into a 'Cispadane Republic'. He had no orders to destroy the Venetian Republic as he did. And he made any return of Lombardy to Austrian rule virtually impossible by creating a new puppet state from French conquests there: the Cisalpine Republic, absorbing the short-lived Cispadane as well as fragments of other territories. From the start, ensconced in semi-regal splendour in the palace of Mombello near Milan, he ruled the new state like a private domain. His only fear was that, as peace talks with the British continued, and the Austrians temporized over finalizing the Leoben settlement, the new majority in the legislative councils and their allies among the directors would negotiate away what he had achieved. The right-wing press in Paris was constantly calling for 'peace without annexations', much to his fury. He started making threats to cross the Alps to save the Republic. Once more, Barras, who had given the untried general his chance two years earlier, and now a director, saw how he could be used. One of his fellow generals in Italy, Charles Pierre François Augereau, was sent home, ostensibly on leave but actually to take command of troops in Paris. With this support, early in September (18 Fructidor in the revolutionary calendar), three of the directors carried through a bloodless coup against the other two and the legislative majority. The leading royalist council members were arrested, the elections of many more were cancelled and journalists who had so enraged Bonaparte were imprisoned. Negotiations with the British were now abruptly broken off, and it became clear to the Austrians that they could equivocate no longer, as Bonaparte threatened to renew the war. Within three months he told the Austrian negotiator he would smash the Habsburg monarchy like so much porcelain. 'I had all the pride of a republican,' he recalled years later, 'and I despised the Austrians.'[5] Only a month after the Fructidor coup, they signed the Peace of Campo Formio, recognizing the loss of Belgium and the legitimacy of the Cisalpine Republic. Venice and assorted German territories were all they received in return. France's Rhine frontier was left to be confirmed by a later imperial congress at Rastatt, but Bonaparte went there in person to ensure that the Republic got what it wanted.

Yet the war was not over. Though left to fight on alone, as war-weary as any of the combatants, the British could not be compelled to surrender as the Austrians had. Only a week before the Peace of Campo Formio was signed, they demonstrated their continued strength with the naval victory of Camperdown, which wiped out a Dutch fleet the French had hoped would redress the balance of power at sea. The British had already used the pretext of the Dutch becoming French satellites to seize key Dutch outposts throughout the world, just as they had earlier descended on most of France's overseas territories. These expeditions were not always as successful as British command of the sea might have presumed, but a blockade on French shipping largely severed any direct trade between France and the colonies she retained, not to mention exports in French ships to the rest of Europe. France could only respond by unleashing privateers against British shipping, but their impact was disappointingly limited.

The obvious course, for a republic now unencumbered by hostilities elsewhere, was to pour its resources into a direct invasion of the British Isles. After all, Hoche's expedition had come within sight of Ireland in December 1796, and a small force had actually disembarked on the Welsh coast a few months later, although the attempt ended in fiasco. The Directory began to assemble an army and transports along the English Channel coasts. Hoche had died suddenly in September 1797, so the returned 'hero of Italy' was given command. He was never enthusiastic. He knew the relative weakness of the French Navy, that its Dutch auxiliary had been destroyed at Camperdown and that the fleet of Spain, now a French ally, had suffered a similar fate at the Battle of St Vincent in the previous February. He also knew that even if the Royal Navy failed to intercept a French invasion, it still might well maroon the invaders (and their general) on a hostile island. Perhaps the directors glimpsed some advantage in that prospect, removing an overmighty general from domestic politics. If so, their reception of his alternative proposal was all the more understandable.

When the Republic of Venice was dismembered at Leoben and Campo Formio, one of the seemingly more eccentric provisions was that France would take over the 'Ionian Islands' of the Adriatic. But, Bonaparte told the Directory before the Fructidor coup,

> The islands of Corfu, Zante and Cephalonia are more interesting for us than the whole of Italy. I believe that if we were obliged to choose, it would be worth more to give Italy back to the emperor and keep the islands, which are a

source of wealth and prosperity for our trade ... The times are not distant when we shall feel that, in order truly to destroy England, we must seize Egypt. The vast Ottoman Empire, declining by the day, makes us obliged to think soon about taking the means to preserve our trade in the Levant.[6]

He found that Talleyrand, the new foreign minister, was having similar thoughts. So the post-Fructidorian directors cannot have been surprised when, in February 1798, the general reported, after a tour of inspection, that the French Navy was in no state to protect an invasion force crossing the English Channel. It would be much better to go to the Levant, 'which would threaten the commerce of India'.[7] Talleyrand, no doubt, took this argument seriously, but for Bonaparte it seems to have been secondary to romantic dreams of conquering the East like a new Alexander. The Mediterranean fleet had been rebuilt since the recapture of Toulon, and there were no British warships in the Mediterranean. No doubt the directors were relieved that the restless general, who had already revealed more than military ambitions, was prepared to leave France for open-ended adventures far away. An expedition to Egypt under his command was rapidly authorized and sailed in May 1798. Bonaparte had always claimed it would be easy, and it was. Malta was seized on the way, and within weeks of landing in Egypt the French had defeated its Mameluke rulers in the Battle of the Pyramids.

Yet the fallout from the Egyptian adventure was disastrous. From the start it was an expedition of conquest. Long gone was any talk of self-defence, or even bringing fraternity and help to peoples aspiring to liberty. The French, including Bonaparte, were now referring to themselves as *la grande nation*, not bound by conventions constraining others. Malta was an independent island state ruled by the Knights of St John; Egypt was a province, however semi-detached, of the Ottoman Empire; it simply suited French interests to appropriate both. But other interests were involved, even for Malta. Czar Paul of Russia considered himself the protector of the knights. The French seizure of the island, together with the earlier annexation of the Venetian islands in the Adriatic, determined him to fight the French, although only two years earlier he had withdrawn from his mother Catherine's anti-French commitments. The unprecedented result was an alliance with the Turks, Russia's traditional enemies and France's traditional friends, to resist French aggression. A week after Bonaparte's victory below the Pyramids, a British fleet hurriedly sent to the Mediterranean under Nelson caught up with the ships that had brought the French to Egypt, anchored in Aboukir Bay. In what the British remember as the Battle of the Nile, they destroyed it, marooning the French land forces. Buoyed by the news, the Turks and Russians formalized their alliance in the presence of British representatives, who offered financial as well as naval support. They also worked feverishly to involve the Austrians.

The emperor had never considered Campo Formio a final settlement of anything, and almost as soon as the treaty was signed, he was making secret overtures to the British. Everything the *grande nation* and its armies did in succeeding months fed Austrian anxieties. A pro-French uprising was engineered in Switzerland, leading to military intervention and the establishment of yet another 'sister republic', the Helvetic, which promptly guaranteed France perpetual access to the Alpine passes into Italy. City republics, like Mulhouse and Geneva, were simply annexed to France, and the whole of Piedmont occupied. In Germany, the Congress of Rastatt finally confirmed the French Rhine frontier. In Italy, the papal states were invaded, the pope arrested and a puppet Roman Republic set up. Thinking the French overstretched against a growing number of enemies, and with their most formidable general and army now cut off in Egypt, the king of Naples decided to come to Rome's rescue. His reward was to be invaded and only rescued by the British fleet, while his mainland kingdom was turned into yet another sister republic. But this made the Russians, whose naval forces had already retaken Bonaparte's coveted Ionian islands, anxious to send troops to Italy. They pressed the emperor to allow them to cross Austrian territory. When he agreed, the French declared war on him. Such an implicitly hostile act left them with little alternative, but it meant that France entered the 1799 campaigning season facing a new coalition of all the great powers except Prussia – determined to stay neutral – and Spain, a fickle and reluctant ally.

This situation was largely of France's own making. The stunning successes of 1797, which had brought even the British as far as the conference table, had made the French arrogant and overconfident. And yet most of the triumphs of that year were the achievement of one man. No other French general had Bonaparte's unbroken record of success, or his consequent ability to dictate the policies of the Republic. Thus it was Bonaparte who devised the unstable settlement of Campo Formio. It was his insistence on annexing the Ionian islands that shook Czar Paul out of his detachment from western European affairs. It was under pressure from Bonaparte that Switzerland was transmuted into a supine sister republic, and Piedmont occupied. It was at his urging that French armies marched on Rome. And all this was before he left for Egypt. Thereafter the seizure of Malta, and Egypt itself, finally brought together a combination of enemies even more formidable than the one France had faced in 1793. Bonaparte had planned to spend no more than a couple of months in the East before returning in renewed triumph. But thanks to Nelson, he and France's most seasoned army were sidelined in ill-informed isolation while most of what he had achieved since 1796 was torn apart.

French forces were seriously overstretched. The number of men under arms had fallen dramatically since the peaks achieved in the twelve months following the *levée en masse*. By 1798 it was down to 325,000. There had been no systematic recruitment since 1794, and casualties, disease and desertion had taken a steady toll. One of the first obligations imposed on every new sister republic was to provide large contingents of soldiers to support their ally and creator. The protection of France, after all, was what these satellites were created for. Yet the French, often with good reason, mistrusted the quality of their auxiliaries. And so, in September 1798, as the international horizon darkened, a comprehensive law of conscription (a new word) was adopted, called the Jourdan Law after the victor of Fleurus who introduced it. All young men between 20 and 25 were made liable to be drafted into the armies. They were classified by the year of their birth, and the government could call up any of the classes thus created according to need. Twenty-year-olds, the class of 1778, were conscripted at once, but the next year, two further classes were called up as well. Initially no exceptions or substitutions were allowed – except that the law was not applied to the nine western departments where the levy of 1793 had triggered still-smouldering insurrections. Yet in the newly annexed departments of the former Austrian Netherlands the same inflammatory circumstances were repeated. Once incorporated into France, this devout region was subjected to the full rigours of the Republic's ecclesiastical policy, with Church lands confiscated, monasteries closed and parish clergy harassed and harried. When, on top of all this, the Jourdan Law introduced conscription, anti-draft riots quickly developed into full-scale rebellion. Unlike the Vendée, it was soon put down, and with ruthless brutality; but still only a quarter of the recruits expected from the Belgian departments had joined the colours by the end of 1799. Even elsewhere the response was patchy.

In the event, the Year VII (beginning September 1798) was not as desperate for the Republic as the Year II, but it was certainly a year of crisis, and in some ways the crisis looked more spectacular.

On every war front, the depleted armies of the Republic were rolled back. All except one of the sister republics established since 1797 collapsed. Two French armies advancing into Germany were thrown back across the Rhine by the Austrians. In Italy, under the overall command of the veteran Russian general Suvorov, allied forces expelled the French from most of the territories conquered by Bonaparte. Mantua, which he had besieged for months in 1796–7, fell to Suvorov after a few weeks. Abandoning Rome and Naples to avoid being cut off, weakened and exposed French armies marched north to further defeat amid widespread popular uprisings against them and their local collaborators. By early summer, French power in Italy had shrunk to a coastal strip around Genoa. Switzerland, too, the French gateway to Italy, was largely lost. On 26 May, weeks before these disasters reached their climax, the Directory ordered the Republic's most successful general to return from Egypt. Intercepted by British warships, the order never reached him; but the disasters that prompted it were the ones reported in the newspapers sent ashore by Sir Sidney Smith in August. Meanwhile his own eastern adventures had been scarcely more successful. His failed siege of Acre had been followed by a harrowing retreat back into Egypt. Italy could surely be held, Bonaparte mused from afar, so long as Mantua held out, but by the time he was back in Egypt Mantua had fallen (28 July).[8] Two days before that, however, he had restored his own endangered reputation by routing the Turkish expeditionary force at Aboukir. He took good care to send full despatches to Paris to announce the scale of his victory, and they got through. Thus he arrived in France in October with his invincible reputation intact.

Yet by then the immediate threat to the Republic was over. The last defeat of the Year VII came on 15 August at Novi, where the Russians even killed Joubert, the latest rising star among French generals. But after that, Russian efforts were redirected northwards into Switzerland, where they were trapped under the Alps by resurgent French armies while their Austrian allies marched off to seek territorial gains along the Rhine. At a series of battles around Zurich in late September the depleted Russians were defeated, although retreating in defiant good order. Nor were the allies any more fortunate further north. An Anglo-Russian expedition against the Batavian Republic launched late in August was checked within a month and withdrew under armistice in the last days of October. In St Petersburg, Czar Paul felt betrayed by his Austrian and British allies. He announced that his alliance with Austria was at an end, and his hitherto warm relations with the British began to cool rapidly. By the time Bonaparte reappeared in France, therefore, the coalition was falling apart. Contrary to his claims then and later, his presence was not necessary to save the Republic from external enemies. Instead, he was able to devote his entire energy and attention to subverting it from within, on his own terms.

* * *

EVEN SO, THE war was far from over. Nor had the new first consul entirely given up in Egypt. He sent messengers to Kléber to reassure him that the French were no longer facing disaster in Europe and began sketching out schemes to put together a relief force. He sent a soothing message to the king of Prussia, hinting that continued neutrality would be rewarded when general peace was concluded. Then on Christmas Day 1799, within days of the new consular constitution coming into force, he wrote open letters to Emperor Francis II and King George III appealing for an end to hostilities. To the emperor he predicted a tripling of casualties in the next campaigning season if war continued. To George III he flattered British power, praised his nation's wisdom and appealed for general pacification of their worldwide quarrels in the name of 'benefiting trade, internal prosperity, and the wellbeing of families'. Published at once in the main newspapers, these letters were directed as much at French public opinion as at their ostensible recipients. Peace was what the French overwhelmingly hoped for from the general now ruling them, and these lofty appeals to enemy monarchs would absolve him of blame if the war went on. They contained no serious proposals, but they showed clearly enough that the first consul recognized what his fellow citizens expected of him. They cut little ice with the rulers they were addressed to. Neither replied directly: diplomatic protocol dictated that monarchs should be addressed only through their ministers. George III, at least, was seriously offended, and the British sent a curt rejection declaring that the best way of restoring peace was to restore the Bourbons to their rightful inheritance. Neither the British nor the Austrians, in any case, could believe that the rule of what William Pitt the Younger called 'this last adventurer in the lottery of Revolutions' would last long.[9] The Austrians reacted more cautiously, and their restraint led to regular informal exchanges with Talleyrand at the French foreign ministry. But Franz Maria von Thugut, the Austrian minister, had no more trust than Pitt in French intentions. He continued to prepare for a new campaign throughout the spring of 1800 and, now formally abandoned by the czar, steadily strengthened his links with the British.

Despite Russia's defection, the Austrian position appeared strong. In Italy, won for them by the energy of Suvorov, they were besieging the last remaining French occupiers in Genoa. In Germany, an army of 120,000 was poised to march across the Rhine into Alsace. With little hope of relieving Genoa directly, the French prepared to confront the main Austrian Army and drive directly towards Vienna. The commander of the French forces was Moreau, who had brought order to the French retreat from Italy the previous summer. The first consul endorsed his plan of campaign, openly declaring that the constitution prohibited him from taking personal command in the field. But the constitution contained no such provision, and privately Bonaparte thought

Moreau's instincts timid and unimaginative. In January he began to organize what he called a 'reserve army' to the east of Switzerland, positioned to strike either north or south of the Alps should the enemy break through. He took care to play down its combat-readiness, and supplies were largely built up in secret. By May 1800, however, it was 60,000 strong. Moreau had begun his campaign in Germany on 25 April, and the Austrians fell steadily back before his advance. A first battle was won at Stokach on 3 May. But in Italy the Austrians launched a final push to take Genoa, and news of this galvanized Bonaparte into action. As word of Stokach arrived, he was preparing to leave Paris to lead the reserve army into action. Within a week he had marched it to the Alps, where it began to cross by the highest and least negotiable of the passes, the Great St Bernard. The first consul picked his own way along the still snowbound route on a sure-footed mule, although posterity was largely persuaded to remember the feat by David's heroic image, painted some time later. The achievement was bold and heroic for all that, and the appearance of a fresh French Army in their rear took the Austrian forces in northern Italy almost completely by surprise. On 2 June, Bonaparte marched in triumph into Milan, as he had four years earlier, emphasizing the message being officially propagated back in Paris: that if he had been in Europe early in 1799, the Republic would never have lost Italy.

Yet it was while he was in Milan that he learnt that Genoa had surrendered. General André Masséna's exhausted garrison had been allowed to march out to French-held territory but was in no physical state to help the first consul's forces. Reinforcements were now arriving across other Alpine passes, but not enough to bring French numbers up to those commanded by the Austrian Field Marshal Melas. With his line of communication cut by the French occupation of Milan, Melas decided to risk a decisive battle while he still enjoyed superiority in infantry, cavalry and artillery. The first consul was also looking for a decisive battle, but initial contacts suggested that the Austrians were covering a withdrawal. He split his forces in the hope of outflanking their retreat. Only late in the morning of 14 June, at Marengo, did he realize that he faced an entire Austrian attacking army. He had not met a well-trained and equipped European adversary for more than three years, let alone with fewer men. Desperately he recalled the units he had detached. Only one, under a trusted Egyptian veteran recently returned, Louis Charles Antoine Desaix, received the order. His return to the main force, with enough men and guns to make the contest more equal, saved the day. A concentrated bombardment, followed by a cavalry onslaught, turned what the Austrians had thought was an advance to victory into a headlong retreat. Although Desaix himself was killed at the head of his troops, a grief-stricken Bonaparte readily acknowledged how much he owed him. If he had lost at Marengo, his mystique of invincibility would have vanished. The consular regime, constructed so recently around his person, might well have collapsed. If peace had followed, it would have been at best without victory.

As it was, the consulate was saved, and so was Bonaparte's career. Nor was the luck, which had always served him so well, at an end. Melas, defeated but still easily strong enough to fight another day, decided instead to seek an armistice. Giving him no time to get authorization from Vienna, the first consul demanded that the Austrians withdraw from all the territories conquered by Suvorov the previous summer. Thugut learnt that Melas had accepted these terms just a day after signing a formal agreement with Great Britain not to conclude a separate peace. Meanwhile, from the battlefield of Marengo itself, the victor addressed a renewed open appeal for peace to Emperor Francis. Why, he asked, had the emperor allowed himself to be misled by the wily British into sacrificing Austria's best interests and so many of the lives of his subjects? He appealed for a return to the peace agreed at Campo Formio and, pending formal negotiations, a general armistice. This at least was

not long in coming. The news of Marengo completed the demor-
alization of the Austrian Army in Germany, steadily retreating
before Moreau's advance. Within a month, again without prior
authorization from Vienna, an armistice was signed at Parsdorf
(15 July). By then, confident that, as he wrote from Milan, 'circumstances are such in Europe, that it is not probable that six months
will pass without peace being concluded', the first consul was back
in Paris, orchestrating lavish victory ceremonies on 14 July, culminating in a parade of wounded survivors from Marengo bearing
captured Austrian flags.[10]

All doubts about his authority within the Republic were now
dispelled. But however much, in all official accounts, the near-
defeat at Marengo was portrayed as yet another effortless victory,
the war went on. Onlookers were surprised at the tepid popular reception for the official celebrations, and the first consul was
certainly aware that only a general peace would satisfy his war-
weary compatriots. All his efforts over the summer were directed
at securing one. Knowing how crucial to the weakening of Austria
the Russian withdrawal from the coalition had been, he showered
Paul 1 with conciliatory gestures, offering to return all Russian
prisoners, and to support the czar's claims to be the protector of
Malta. The French garrison there, a relic of the 1798 Egyptian expedition, was still blockaded by the Royal Navy, and looked likely
to fall soon. It did so on 5 September. The British occupation
that followed was the last straw in Paul 1's deteriorating relations
with London. He now redoubled efforts, begun over the previous
winter, to revive an idea first tried in 1782, an 'Armed Neutrality'
of the north, designed to exclude British shipping from the Baltic.
All this, the French hoped, might spur the British to open peace
talks. Informal overtures had in fact been made throughout the
spring by Louis Guillaume Otto, a commissioner maintained in
London by the Republic for exchanging prisoners of war. After
the Austrian armistices, Otto was instructed to propose a parallel

naval armistice with Great Britain. Dominating the seas as completely as they did, the British spurned the idea. They knew in any case that Thugut was determined to honour the alliance and that he was using the continental armistices to prepare a new campaign.

But Thugut's control of Austrian policy was slipping. The armistices in Italy and Germany had been concluded without reference to him. Then later in July, an envoy sent to Paris to confirm the ceasefire took it upon himself, perhaps somewhat browbeaten by Bonaparte and Talleyrand, to negotiate a complete set of peace preliminaries based, as the first consul had suggested to the emperor, on the terms of Campo Formio. It was stipulated that should these terms be rejected, full-scale war would resume on 15 August. Wrong-footed again by a subordinate, the emperor and his minister were able to reject these terms on the grounds that they were treaty-bound to the British not to conclude a separate peace. But, in order to prolong the armistice, they suggested opening exploratory talks in the presence of a British observer. The French agreed and proposed an extended truce subject to the surrender of Austrian-held strongpoints in Bavaria. Without consulting Thugut, Francis ii accepted. An enraged Thugut resigned, while his successor Johann Ludwig von Cobenzl, who had previously negotiated with Bonaparte at Campo Formio and thought he knew his man, travelled to France to open negotiations. But Cobenzl now found himself dealing not with a general but a head of state. He was loftily received, and, not bending immediately to determined psychological pressure, was packed off to Lunéville, in distant Lorraine, to discuss terms with the consul's elder brother Joseph. Barely had he reached Lunéville than Moreau was authorized to renew the campaign in Germany. This time it only lasted a matter of weeks. On 3 December, at Hohenlinden, Moreau routed the main Austrian Army and pursued its remnants towards Vienna. In Italy, other French armies began to push the imperial forces back beyond the lines agreed after Marengo. The desperate Austrians begged for a ceasefire on both fronts. At Lunéville, Cobenzl abandoned his insistence that nothing could be settled without the British. Neither was he any longer in a position to bargain over the terms that France was offering him. A definitive peace was signed there on 9 February 1801.

Hohenlinden was an altogether more convincing and decisive victory than Marengo. It ended the war on the continent in complete triumph. At Lunéville, France's Rhine frontier was confirmed, and the French sister republics in northern Italy and Switzerland were resurrected. Austria retained Venice and its Adriatic dependencies as at Campo Formio, but the emperor's brother the Grand Duke of Tuscany was obliged to retire to a shrunken apanage in Germany, his former dukedom now blended with the duchy of Parma into a new kingdom of Etruria. This had already been secretly promised by France the previous October to Charles IV of Spain in the Convention of San Ildefonso: his son-in-law was to succeed to the new kingdom in return for Spain handing over the vast North American territory of Louisiana to the French Republic. It was the first sign that Bonaparte was thinking about restoring a French transatlantic empire. It was also the first time that the Republic had created a client monarchy rather than a sister republic – and for a Bourbon, no less. The Bourbons of Naples, the last relics of the coalition, were also relieved when the triumphant French forces in Italy, instead of invading afresh, simply imposed a peace treaty on them in March which left their kingdom intact but garrisoned by French forces in three of its key naval ports. Privately, the first consul was reserving the option of deposing the Neapolitan Bourbons in the future, but for the moment he was content to destroy their alliance with the British.

All this he claimed credit for. He had toyed with striking the final blow himself, at the head of the armies in Germany but, in the event, that glory fell to Moreau. Although Moreau had willingly stood aside in October 1799 to let Bonaparte be Sieyès' 'sword', the two generals had never been close, and Hohenlinden made them military rivals. The victor of Italy had no high opinion of the other's talents but felt obliged to flatter him and publicly sing his praises. Moreau, however, kept his distance. He refused an offer to join the Bonaparte clan by marrying Joséphine's daughter, Hortense. After Hohenlinden, he was never given another command by the ruler whose power he had done so much to establish.

This time, Paris welcomed the news of peace more wholeheartedly. It had been brought to the entire continent through total French victory. There was a month of celebrations, receptions, fireworks, parades. The consular government ceaselessly proclaimed that only British obstinacy stood in the way of general European peace. The British were indeed obstinate, and over the spring of 1801 they flexed their muscles impressively. Although appalled by the collapse of their Austrian ally, by the time the Lunéville treaty was signed they had launched an expedition to Egypt to deal with the French forces left there. Initially this was hazardous. During the armistices with Austria, the French had succeeded in putting together a relieving force which sailed from Brest as far as Toulon, eluding the British Atlantic blockade. When it finally sailed, however, it was too late. The British were ashore in Egypt, backed by superior naval forces. It only took them a few months to defeat the poorly led and demoralized remnants of a once-impressive French force, which finally surrendered in September. By then, too, British seapower had blown apart the Armed Neutrality of the North by destroying the Danish fleet blocking the entrance to the Baltic at Copenhagen (2 April). And only a few days earlier the architect and animator of the Armed Neutrality, Paul i of Russia, had been assassinated in St Petersburg. Bonaparte's wooing of the czar had been beginning to bear fruit, not just in the Armed Neutrality, but in the brusque expulsion of Louis XVIII from the Russian refuge he had found since 1798. The first consul was understandably devastated when news of the murder arrived and blamed a British plot. He cannot have been so surprised when, within a few months, the new Czar Alexander moved to restore good relations with London.

Yet by then, too, France's own relations with London were quietly improving. Once again chance came to Bonaparte's aid. In February 1801 for reasons that had nothing to do with the fortunes of war against France, William Pitt resigned as British prime minister. Confronted by the refusal of George III to admit Catholics to parliament, which Pitt had tacitly promised in order to win Irish Catholic support for the legislative union of Great Britain and Ireland introduced in 1801, the prime minister felt honour-bound to leave office. He carried with him the leading ministers who had planned and conducted the war against France. And although the new ministry of Henry Addington took office against the background of amphibious and naval triumphs in Egypt and the Baltic, they had no illusions about what was expected of them. With France in complete control of the continent, there was no prospect of overall victory. Popular discontent with the burdens of almost ten years of disappointing conflict was made worse by the consequences of a bad harvest in 1799, with high bread prices and a knock-on fall in industrial demand and rising unemployment throughout 1800. These problems were exacerbated by disruptions to Baltic trade caused by the Armed Neutrality. That winter witnessed widespread rioting across the British Isles, and parliament was deluged with petitions. Troops were widely deployed to maintain order. 'Was not the war', proclaimed a subversive meeting in Yorkshire in April 1801, 'the cause of all present calamities?'[11]

Although no more convinced than in 1798 that a successful invasion of the British Isles was a serious possibility, Bonaparte ordered a military build-up along the Channel coast to foment further alarm on the other side. He knew by then that the new ministry in London had resumed informal peace feelers through Otto, and that they had offered terms that looked almost like surrender. This only encouraged Bonaparte to ask for more. He demanded to keep Egypt, no doubt to expunge the shame of having abandoned it two years earlier. But even as he made these demands, French armies on the Nile were facing defeat, and the new British foreign secretary, Robert Banks Jenkinson, Lord Hawkesbury, refused to countenance their remaining in this potential gateway to India.

Yet British desperation to make peace was becoming increasingly obvious. It was now widely known on both sides of the Channel that negotiations were under way, and public expectations were rising. Never a patient man, the first consul was now thinking ahead, to post-war projects, and by mid-September he could no longer wait. 'Before going to Marengo', he told Otto,

> the First Consul offered everything to the Emperor: he had, as he does today with England, offered everything compatible with honour. The Emperor wanted more, and he was obliged to obtain what he could get from the generosity and the moderation of the victor. Any request for new instructions from you is useless from today; you must tell Lord Hawkesbury so, and let him know that what you have said to him is an ultimatum; that the First Consul would risk everything rather than go further; and say that with some pride: they risk losing everything, just like the Emperor, if they wish to have more.[12]

Much of this, the British must have seen, was bluster; but increasingly Addington was counting the ruinous cost of fighting on. Urged on even by Pitt, and supported by the king, on 10 October he agreed to the signature of peace preliminaries.

The terms of the preliminaries broadly recognized that while France dominated the continent, Britain ruled the waves. France tacitly acknowledged that Egypt was lost, but was satisfied to accept its reversion to Turkish rule. In return for French troops evacuating the ports of southern Italy, the British agreed to abandon Malta to the Knights of St John. France offered no other concessions. Bonaparte's line was that what had been agreed at Lunéville and after between continental powers was none of Britain's business. On the other hand, his power was such that he could compel his continental allies and satellites to deliver enough overseas losses to make peace worthwhile to the islanders. Thus the Batavian Republic would allow Britain to keep captured bases in Ceylon, and Spain must give up Trinidad to its British occupiers. London, however, agreed to return the Cape of Good Hope to the Dutch, Minorca to Spain, and Martinique and other captured outposts to France. So none of Britain's original war aims had been achieved. The French Republic's legitimacy was implicitly recognized, and George III now even gave up the historic claim of English monarchs, going back to the fourteenth century, to be kings of France. French domination of the low countries, prevention of which was the most long-standing and fundamental of British interests in Europe, was also conceded. It was true that the war had crippled French commercial competition, but peace opened the way for its revival, as Bonaparte intended. By contrast, France's war aims since 1793 had been triumphantly achieved. The treaty of Lunéville had established the 'natural' frontier of the Rhine and added a buffer zone of satellite states. Peace with Great Britain offered implicit recognition of this achievement by the last power to resist it.

Hostilities ended at once. It was now too late for France to save its forces in Egypt, but the seas were open again, and within days of agreeing the preliminaries, the first consul was organizing a fleet to sail to the Caribbean to reimpose metropolitan rule on Saint-Domingue and repossess the other sugar islands to be relinquished by the British. British protests that this was premature were brushed aside. Negotiation of a definitive treaty was entrusted by the British side to Marquis Cornwallis, who had more experience as a soldier and administrator than as a diplomat. The French chief negotiator, as at Lunéville, was Joseph Bonaparte, his brother's obedient but more emollient mouthpiece. Before proceeding to the negotiating table at Amiens, Cornwallis waited on the first consul in Paris. He found him, he reported to Hawkesbury, 'gracious to the highest degree', but to a friend he was more open.[13] 'I had two interviews with Bonaparte ... He is quick, animated, *et il parle en Roi*. In talking of public affairs, where France is concerned, the language is, "I would rather give up; it is hard upon me ... &c. &c."'[14]

In Amiens, Cornwallis soon found he had more to do than fill in a few final details of the preliminaries. Bonaparte deployed his usual tactics of treating an agreement as an opening bid and threatening to walk out if consent was not secured to what he wished. His brother and Cornwallis got along well personally, but neither had much freedom of action. After months of talks, little progress had been made, Cornwallis complaining that what was agreed one day might always be repudiated the next. The French appear to have been spinning things out until their Caribbean fleet had sailed unhindered, and until the first consul, at a congress of Italian collaborators in Lyon, had consolidated the Cisalpine Republic by changing its name to Italian and having himself declared its president. His spokesmen at Amiens began to raise new issues not covered in the preliminaries, such as complaints over attacks on the first consul by émigré French journalists in London. Above all the two sides could not agree on details concerning the timetable for the British evacuation of Malta. By March 1802 the British were becoming desperate and contemplating a breakdown of the talks. Crews of warships expecting to be decommissioned, but then ordered to shadow the French Caribbean expedition, mutinied. Addington was anxious that continued uncertainties were about to dry up his government's financial credit. Yet the first consul no more desired a breakdown of talks than he did. He wanted to seal the triumph promised by the preliminaries, and to show that, single-handedly, he had brought peace to the whole of Europe. Quite suddenly, in mid-March, his intransigence melted away, and, like the British ministry, he tacitly allowed outstanding issues to remain unresolved. Dutch and Spanish representatives were present at Amiens to sign off on what the French had surrendered or won back on their behalf, so the peace could be presented as general. All signed on 27 March 1802.

Nobody in Great Britain called the peace a triumph. But even Pitt commended it as the best deal that could be imagined, most military and naval commanders agreed, and it was ratified in both Houses of Parliament by overwhelming majorities. 'Do you know what I call the Peace?' exclaimed George III, '*an experimental Peace*, for it is nothing else ... It was unavoidable.'[15] Most of his subjects were less equivocal. The preliminaries had been greeted with euphoria as promising lower taxes and the end of a decade of hardship. Merchants and manufacturers looked forward to a reopening of trade with the continent and hoped for a return to the Anglo-French commercial treaty of 1786.

There would be no question of that. Even as he arrived in Amiens, an industrial town, to open the talks, Joseph Bonaparte had written to his brother that 'the workers who make up a very numerous class, were extremely upset by the idea of a new commercial treaty, or by the renewal of that of 1786. I reassured them.'[16] These were the only apprehensions aroused in France by the Peace. Everywhere else there was spectacular public rejoicing at the definitive ending of the war. Symbolically, the first consul appeared in public in civilian clothes for the first time since Marengo, to receive the congratulations of a grateful nation. As Antoine-Claire Thibaudeau, one-time regicide deputy but now a trusted councillor of state, put it, 'He had made peace, not by necessity, like England, but because the French people were calling for it with all their might, [and] because it was glorious for France.'[17] Although nothing explicit was said in the treaty, like the preliminaries it also implied British acceptance of the terms of Lunéville, the ultimate recognition of the first consul's triumph on European battlefields, and so the victorious end of the wars of the French Revolution. As always, the man himself saw his triumph as something more, and he was right. Immediately after Marengo, he told a Prussian diplomat that

> Every day peace is becoming more necessary for Europe. It is not sufficiently realized that the French Revolution is not over so long as the scourge of war goes on, and that this Revolution can still disturb, shake and overturn many states as it continues. I want peace, as much to establish the present French government, as to save the world from chaos.[18]

Talleyrand, whose part in orchestrating peace negotiations was more substantial than the first consul ever chose to acknowledge, agreed: 'It could be said without the least exaggeration,' he wrote in his memoirs, that

> at the Peace of Amiens, France abroad enjoyed power, glory and influence such that the most ambitious mind could desire nothing more for his country. And what rendered this situation even more marvellous was the rapidity with which it had been brought about ... France had gone from the degradation into which the Directory had plunged her, to the first rank in Europe. It might be thought that [the first consul] had put an end to the Revolution.[19]

Yet this encomium was not without its subtle reservations. Talleyrand knew there was never an occasion when his former master was not dreaming of more. The ink on what he called *his* peace was scarcely dry before he was speculating on how long it might last. All the other powers hated France, he told Thibaudeau.[20] They must be cowed, and soon, by new victories. 'In our position,' he declared, 'I regard every peace as a short truce; yet don't believe that I would wish to break the peace: no, I shall not play the part of aggressor. I have too great an interest in leaving the initiative to foreigners. I know them well; they will be the first to take up arms again or to provide me with just reasons to take them up . . . my principle is, war is better than ephemeral peace.' The war he had just won had been launched by a revolutionary nation. The ones he looked forward to would be his alone.

SIGNATURE DU CONCORDAT.

Entre le Gouvernement Français et sa Sainteté Pie VII. Pour le rétablissement du Culte Catholique en France.

1. Joseph Bonaparte. 2. Le Cardinal Gonsalvi. 3. Joseph Archevêque de Corinthe. 4. Crétet, Conseiller d'État. 5. Bernier Prêtre François. 6. Cacelli Prêtre Romain.

A Paris chez Basset, Md. d'Estampes et Fabricant de Papiers peints Rue S.t Jacques N.o 64.

Anonymous, 'Signature of the Concordat', 1801, engraving.

3

Treating with God

'I am very glad not to have a religion,' declared the dying Napoleon. 'It is a great consolation: I have no fearful illusions, I fear nothing that lies ahead.'[1] Raised by his mother as an orthodox Catholic, when very young he had been an altar boy. But he had lost his faith, he recalled, at the age of eleven, on hearing from the pulpit that virtuous heroes who had lived before the time of Christ were destined to burn in hell.[2] He never doubted that God had created the world but was sure that He did not intervene there. 'What has the divine law to do with human matters?' The seventeen-year-old subaltern mused in 1786.[3] The clergy's kingdom was not of this world yet its claims to independent divine authority made it a perpetual threat to the unity of the state. The clergy preached obedience and acceptance of poverty, 'but the power that drives their institution says, "Be rich!"'

Such opinions were common enough among the generation that would make the French Revolution. The clergy were not popular. The cahiers of 1789, those grievance-lists drawn up by electors to the Estates-General to guide the work of their chosen representatives, were full of complaints about the unearned, untaxed wealth of the Church, its uneven distribution among the clergy and the privileges they enjoyed. Idle monks and canons were denounced as leading worthless lives, often sustained by tithes impropriated from the parish priests they were meant to remunerate. Absentee courtier bishops neglected their flocks to live high on revenues swollen by pluralism, while more zealous prelates devoted more energy to doctrinal quarrelling and persecution than pastoral care of the laity. Nobody thought that a reforming Revolution, when it came, would leave the Church untouched. But few foresaw how far-reaching its attempts to purge the Church of abuses would be.

The clergy played an essential role in the establishment of the Revolution. The regulations for election to the Estates-General were deliberately framed to swell the representation of parish priests in the clerical delegation, and they did. Seventy per cent of its chosen members were ordinary parish priests and, though instinctively deferential to their episcopal superiors, many among them sympathized with the deputies of the Third Estate into which they had been born. They mistrusted aristocratic prelates who tried to align the clergy with the noble delegation's defence of privilege. Eventually a handful of parish priests broke the separatist solidarity of the first two orders and joined the Third Estate in proclaiming the National Assembly and the sovereignty of the nation on 17 June 1789. And the instigator of this founding revolutionary movement was himself a priest, though sitting for the Third Estate: none other than Sieyès, who a decade later would begin the process that brought the Revolution to an end.

The destiny of Sieyès was to find himself repeatedly disappointed by what the Revolution brought about; and the first disappointment came barely seven weeks after the National Assembly proclaimed itself. On the Night of 4 August the parish clergy were abruptly deprived of their livelihoods when tithes were abolished without compensation. Sieyès thought this an affront to property rights, but most clergy were more concerned about how, in future, they would be paid. Vestry fees, a more variable source of income, were also abolished in the wave of renunciations and suppressions on that euphoric night; and when some clergy protested, they were met with threats that the entire property of the Church ought to be sequestered, on the grounds that it was merely held in trust from the nation. Within three months sequestration happened: on

2 November, on the motion of Talleyrand, then the young bishop of Autun, the lands of the Church were declared to be 'at the disposal' of the nation so that they could be sold off to settle the debt which had brought the Revolution about. And in the meantime the clergy had lost a struggle to retain the Church's spiritual monopoly. The Declaration of the Rights of Man and the Citizen of 26 August proclaimed complete freedom of thought and opinion 'even religious'. The whole age-old structure of the Gallican Church was being torn down, and its powers shrivelled. Loss of lands in turn threatened the viability of major institutions such as chapters and monasteries. It was no coincidence that the first sale of Church lands authorized by the assembly on 19 December came in a decree that released all religious from their vows. Wholesale dissolution of monasteries followed in February, evoking echoes of the Reformation; and more paranoid clerics began to speculate that the entire Revolution was some sort of Protestant plot. To reassure themselves and the nation, in April 1790, a devout group of deputies backed a motion by the Carthusian monk Dom Gerle to declare Roman Catholicism the state religion, with a monopoly of public worship. After two days of bitter debate, the motion was defeated.

All this had taken place with hardly any recognition that the French Church was part of a wider confession. The pope in Rome was not consulted about any of it. A long tradition of 'Gallicanism' had always resisted the pope's jurisdictional claims over the French church, acknowledging his supremacy only over doctrine. Ever since the Concordat of Bologna in 1516, French canon lawyers had vaunted the superiority of royal authority in other matters. The National Assembly now saw itself as inheriting that authority. For all their claims to institutional independence, the French clergy had always paid annates, the first year's revenue of benefices, towards the upkeep of the Holy See. But annates were discontinued in the torrent of abolition and renunciation on the night of

4 August. Rome did not react, even when the anti-clerical drift of events in France prompted inhabitants of Avignon, an enclave of papal territory, to agitate for absorption into the sovereign nation. But when, in May 1789, the Ecclesiastical Committee of the National Assembly produced proposals for the future organization of a Church shorn of most of its former revenues and organization, Pius VI could scarcely avoid taking a stand.

The Civil Constitution of the Clergy redrew the ecclesiastical map, diminishing the number of benefices and dioceses to produce a more equal and rational distribution which reflected the nation's reformed administrative structure. All incumbents under the new order were to receive respectable salaries from the state, but all must actively fulfil their priestly duties, and all were to be elected, just like civil officials, by 'active' citizens qualified only by levels of wealth, not faith. Thus Protestants and Jews might be involved in choosing Catholic priests, whereas the pope was assigned no involvement at all, at any level. He was merely to be informed as a courtesy. These were radical departures from the historic structures and procedures of the Catholic Church, although their supporters claimed they were merely returning the church to its primitive simplicity and purity. More pragmatic bishops thought that they might nevertheless prove broadly acceptable, provided that the Church, as a whole, was consulted. But the Assembly of the sovereign nation would not hear of that. Nobody affected by its other reforms had been consulted about them, and to treat the Church as a special case would be to revive the privileged status it had lost in 1789. Denied a voice of its own for the first time in its history, the Church of France was compelled to look for authoritative guidance from what even the civil constitution designated as 'the visible head of the universal Church'.

Though appalled from the start by the drift of events in France, Pius VI still carefully avoided public comment for fear of making matters worse. Privately he urged Louis XVI to seek ways of blunting the impact of the Assembly's policies on the Church but said nothing more openly. Even when the civil constitution was complete, and he urged the king to veto it so as not to plunge the nation into schism, he maintained public silence. But by now, Louis XVI's fixed policy was to veto nothing, and the papal entreaties were ignored. The Civil Constitution came into force, with only the king and his ministers knowing about the hostility of the universal church's visible head.

The result was massive confusion. There was widespread resistance to the redrawing of parish and diocesan boundaries, particularly among incumbents whose benefices were to disappear. And when sees or parishes fell vacant through death, there was uncertainty about procedures for replacing incumbents. Civic authorities, newly elected just months beforehand, were often hesitant and unclear about how they should apply the law. Meanwhile nothing was clarified by the increasingly ominous silence from Rome. Outraged that there should be any doubt about its authority and intentions, the Assembly decided to outlaw ambiguity. On 27 November 1790 it decreed that all ecclesiastics must take a public oath of fidelity to the nation, the law and the king, and swear to uphold with all their power the constitution decreed by the National Assembly and accepted by the king. Those who failed to take this oath would be deprived of their benefices, their civil rights and future eligibility for public functions. They were explicitly branded 'perturbers of the public peace'.

The king took a month to accept the decree as he desperately urged the pope to make some conciliatory gesture. The royal delay, and continued papal silence, only served to envenom the atmosphere when, as 1791 began, priests confronted swollen congregations anxious to see how they swore. The results were astounding, not least for a National Assembly expecting widespread, even if reluctant, compliance. Around half the clergy refused. Less than a third even of clerical deputies in the assembly took the oath, and only seven bishops, among them the ever-pragmatic Talleyrand. And it was not only the clergy who were polarized. All the faithful were now obliged to decide whether they should accept the sacraments from priests who had chosen, or not, to yield to the will of the nation rather than await the consent of the Church. The oath did not specifically mention the civil constitution. It pledged allegiance to the whole constitution, as yet unfinished, but destined to incorporate the ecclesiastical settlement. In any case, it promised obedience to the law, and the Civil Constitution had now been duly passed and sanctioned. The confusions and hesitations of the previous autumn had already alerted the forces of patriotism to the anti-revolutionary potential of clerical opposition, and now they mobilized to promote oath-taking. National guardsmen attended the occasions to keep order, but they were not always able, or even inclined, to prevent intimidation and occasional physical violence against nonjurors. Over the spring, there was a dramatic rise in the number and membership of Jacobin clubs, stimulated by the need to support the 'constitutional' church of oath-takers. And, in spite of widespread, if uneven, resistance, it steadily began to establish itself. A crucial moment came on 24 February, when two bishops, elected under the new rules, were consecrated, thus maintaining the apostolic succession. The celebrant was Talleyrand, whose repeated treachery to his cloth Rome would always find hard to forgive.

This act of defiance was not yet known in Rome when Pius VI finally broke his silence with a brief (*Quod aliquantum*, 10 March) which condemned the entire religious policy of the National Assembly. A covering letter to the king accused him of weakness and failure to honour his own coronation oath to protect the Church. The brief had not yet been made public in France when the pope learnt of the constitutional consecrations. For once, the papal curia responded quickly. A second brief (*Charitas*, 13 April) condemned the election of priests and bishops, oath-taking and unauthorized consecrations. All clergy involved were required to retract or have their priestly powers revoked. With this brief, the Holy See declared spiritual war on the French Revolution and all its works.

* * *

NOW THAT THE pope had spoken, no French Catholic could any longer avoid the unenviable choice. From this moment, the nation was polarized. By making religious allegiance the touchstone of loyalty to the Revolution and its work, the Constituent Assembly opened up the first great divide since 1789, and one which would poison the course of events for more than a decade. And almost at once it helped to create a second great divide, on the issue of monarchy. Louis XVI was conventionally devout. He was stung by the pope's accusation that he had broken his coronation oath to protect the Church. He was now determined to take his Easter communion of 1791 from a nonjuring or 'refractory' priest in private, beyond the publicity of the capital, where support for the oath-taking clergy was strong. But a hostile and suspicious crowd, supported by members of the National Guard, prevented him from leaving, and his reaction was to bring forward plans for permanent escape which had been in gestation since the previous October. In the open letter of justification, which he left behind on his ill-fated Flight to Varennes on 21 June, the king denounced the Revolution's religious policy and complained that he had been forced against his will to attend a constitutional mass. Consequently, the widespread republicanism, which came into the open after his attempted escape, was also suffused with suspicion towards nonjuring priests. Rome and royalism began to come together as inseparable sources of counter-revolution.

Embarrassed and shaken by the extent of oath-refusal among the clergy, which received a new boost when the papal position was made clear, the Assembly sought at first to allow nonjurors and their congregations to worship freely in accordance with the Declaration of the Rights of Man and the Citizen. It even encouraged dispossessed incumbents to continue their ministry until 'constitutional' replacements could be found. But nonjuror priests struggled stubbornly to retain the loyalty of their flocks, obstructed the handover of their churches to constitutional 'intruders' denounced as schismatics, and did all they could to discourage the sale of nationalized Church property. Civil authorities attempting to support constitutional inductions met widespread resistance. Many of the deputies elected over the summer to the Legislative Assembly, which convened in October, had served as local officials and had learnt in that capacity how troublesome recalcitrant priests could be. A final conciliatory gesture of the departing Constituent Assembly was to exclude the Civil Constitution of the Clergy from the new constitution itself, thus making it easier for clerics to take the oath. But relations with Rome were further blighted when, three weeks before it dispersed, the assembly voted to annex the papal territory of Avignon.

Thus the Legislative Assembly convened in a mood of exasperation with religious turmoil. And now there were only a handful of clerical deputies to speak up on spiritual matters, all, by definition, constitutional oath-takers. When reports arrived, in the following weeks, of violent clashes in the Vendée and elsewhere in the west as constitutional intruders were imposed on refractory parishes, the new legislators decided that further action was needed. Isolated proposals to solve the problem by repealing the Civil Constitution altogether were brushed aside, and after several days of impassioned debate, on 29 November 1791, the Assembly denounced refractory priests as threats to public order and security, who used religion as a pretext for obstructing the work of the Revolution. They were now required to demonstrate their respect for the law by publicly taking a fresh oath of loyalty to the constitution, on pain of loss of pension rights, deportation from their place of residence and imprisonment, if convicted of incitement to defy the law. They were also to be denied access to any church or former church.

The king vetoed the decree, ostensibly in the interests of not further polarizing the nation. But his action only served to bring refractories and royalism even closer together. And the link between international Catholicism and counter-revolution stood out from the hospitality offered by German prince-archbishops to the king's émigré brothers and their growing band of aristocratic expatriates. When war broke out against the Habsburg emperor in the spring of 1792, the pope gave the imperial side his open support, urging the emperor to take back Avignon for the Holy See and restore true religion in France. This made nonjurors, who seemingly preferred the authority of the pope to that of the nation, look like potential traitors. Ominously, too, suspicion of priest-craft in general was beginning to affect even the constitutional church: on 6 April the wearing of clerical dress was forbidden. Constitutional bishops in the assembly ostentatiously removed their skullcaps and pectoral crosses, but this reduction to public anonymity scarcely rewarded oath-takers for their commitment to the Revolution.

Renewed attempts to curb nonjuror subversion marked the first disastrous weeks of the war. It was now decreed that any nonjuror might be deported on the petition of twenty active citizens. But once again the king used his veto, and stalemate followed until the fall of the monarchy on 10 August. At local level, however, the royal veto was often ignored as patriotic officials, urged on by Jacobin clubs, stepped up harassment of nonjurors and their flocks. After 10 August the Assembly threw its full weight behind them, and the law took effect without the need for royal sanction. Yet now it no longer seemed enough. Within days of the republican revolution, a new civic oath was devised making no mention of the king, but pledging allegiance to the nation, liberty and equality, and willingness to die in their defence. All public officials, and all priests, were required to take it. Overriding all previous oaths, it offered the opportunity for a new start, and some eminent refractories, even among those now in bitter exile, thought it acceptable. Their equivocations were soon eclipsed by the massacres of early September in Paris. Beginning with an attack on a batch of nonjurors being conveyed to prison, four days of bloodletting left 223 priests dead, between a fifth and a quarter of the victims. Nonjuring now had its martyrs, and the bond between it and the fallen monarchy had been sealed with their blood.

* * *

SO THE REPUBLIC, officially proclaimed on 20 September 1792, began its life at war with the Roman Catholic Church. While the pope urged the monarchs of Europe to unite to restore Louis XVI to his throne, and Avignon to his own rule, there was a massive surge in clerical emigration from France. More than 30,000 priests, monks and nuns left the country in the ensuing months, while the dwindling body of nonjurors remaining were forced into hiding. In January 1793 the execution of the king, who was granted a priest for his last moments, gave nonjuring its most distinguished martyr of all. And when, only weeks later, full-blown domestic armed resistance to the Republic burst out in the Vendée, the rebels fought under the slogan of Church and King. Priests came out of hiding to inspire them, and, when captured, suffered the only possible penalty. Priestly captives from the Vendée were so numerous in Nantes by November 1793 they began to be executed, not by the guillotine but in mass drownings in the Loire – the notorious *noyades*. Others, condemned to deportation, died in pestiferous hulks moored at La Rochelle and Rochefort. By the summer of 1793 rebellion against the Republic had spread to major provincial cities, and here, too, nonjurors reappeared in public to inspire defiance. But by the end of the year, the Republic was back in control and wreaking vengeance with terror. Between March 1793 and August 1794 around a thousand death sentences were imposed on clergy by revolutionary courts, and many more must have died in prison or through unrecorded lawlessness.

Nor, by this stage, were all the clerical victims of revolutionary justice or vengeance nonjurors. The early months of the Republic also witnessed the abandonment of the constitutional church of oath-takers. Refractory resistance to the new religious organization had thrown suspicion on priests of all sorts. Thus, on the very last day of the Legislative Assembly, in a session which also saw the legalization and secularization of divorce, the clergy were deprived of their traditional function of registering births, marriages and deaths. And although more priests were elected to the new legislature, the Convention, than to its predecessor, they soon found themselves expected to give a lead in diluting the doctrinal and canonical character of a church defined by a superseded old order and more detached than ever from the spiritual authority of Rome. Nothing defied that authority more spectacularly than renunciation of celibacy. Occasional clerical marriages had taken place before 1792 but now they were positively encouraged and applauded as signs of republican loyalty. A first constitutional bishop took a wife as early as November 1792, and by the end of the Convention, between 4,500 and 6,000 priests had done the same. Such repudiations of the essence of Catholic priesthood did nothing to stem the dwindling loyalty of the laity, and in the face of ever-shrinking congregations, more and more constitutional clergy simply abjured their orders entirely. Eventually around 20,000 did so. By the middle of 1793 it was often in response to official pressure, in the form of a widespread campaign of complete dechristianization.

Although uneven in its application and impact, this was the first attempt in world history to stamp out all religious practice. It developed as the Republic confronted Catholic enemies abroad and widespread internal rebellion. A trickle of steadily more punitive measures against priestly suspects and public displays of religious commitment culminated in the establishment of a republican calendar, with ten-day weeks and no provision for traditional Sundays. By October certain deputies sent out on mission to the departments were imposing their own strict anti-religious policies. Most notorious, because of its later influence and, in retrospect, the identity of its instigator, was the campaign of Joseph Fouché in the Nièvre. Later Napoleon's most notorious police minister, Fouché was himself a former priest who abandoned his cloth by marrying in November 1792. In the Nièvre he ordered all priests to marry or adopt children and forced a constitutional bishop and thirty of his clergy publicly to renounce their orders. He ordered all religious signs to be removed from public view, and the gates of graveyards to bear the legend *Death is an eternal sleep*. 'Fanaticism', he boasted to the Committee of Public Safety in Paris, with no sense of irony, 'is struck down.'[4]

The committee was less than happy about such extremism but unable, for the moment, to rein it in. Other representatives on mission were pursuing similar policies, sometimes inspired by Fouché's example. Also inspired, on a visit to his native Nièvre, was the procurator of the Paris commune Anaxagoras Chaumette. On his return to the capital in October 1793 he promoted plunder of all churches, culminating in a notorious Festival of Reason in Notre Dame on 10 November. Three days earlier the constitutional bishop of Paris, Jean-Baptiste Gobel, had come before the Convention to renounce his see and his orders, throw off his pectoral cross and don the red cap of liberty. Several priest-deputies followed his example, but one did not. Henri Grégoire, constitutional bishop of Blois, who later coined a new word in denouncing the plunder of churches as 'vandalism', declared that he saw no conflict between liberty and his episcopal duties to his flock. Clad defiantly in clerical dress, he spurned the jeers of other deputies and the public galleries. Almost single-handedly he would later keep the remnants of the constitutional church alive over the rest of the revolutionary decade.

There was little sign of that in the weeks that followed as, all over the country, churches were closed, festivals of reason proliferated and religion was mocked and lampooned in blasphemous charades. By the end of 1793 public Christian worship had almost disappeared throughout the Republic and reprisals for defeated rebels, priests to the fore, were reaching their height. But leading deputies were worried. The clergy might be decimated, perhaps deservedly, but the religious instincts and loyalties of most ordinary citizens appeared largely intact, and resentful of dechristianizing excesses. Both Robespierre and Danton, leading spokesmen for the new republican order, warned against the alienating effects of 'atheism', and early in December the Convention was persuaded to condemn any violence contravening religious freedom. Aware of widespread outbreaks of lay resistance to the closure and plunder of churches, and the spread of defiant religious assemblies even without priests, Robespierre began to ponder how to harness persistent popular religiosity to the cause of the Revolution. His solution, proposed early in May 1794 and inaugurated in a grandiose public ceremony on 8 June, was the Cult of the Supreme Being. Years later, looking back, Napoleon thought Robespierre deserved credit for trying to address the reality of his compatriots' persistent religious instincts. And initially the cult proved quite popular, less perhaps because it was a satisfactory substitute for the Church than because it was thought to herald the end of terror. So far from that, it coincided with the last and most indiscriminately destructive phase of public slaughter in Paris. The Cult of the Supreme Being was in effect dechristianization by other means, and it did not long survive its designer's overthrow a mere six weeks later. Nor, accordingly, did the previous cult of atheistic reason. The religious terror might be over, but it had not destroyed religion. In fact, it left the faithful more bitterly determined than ever at the memories of its atrocities. The problem of how the Republic should deal with religion remained unresolved.

The immediate reflex was to disengage completely. In the last days of the Year II (18 September 1794) the constitutional clergy were at last disowned. The Convention, on an ostensible financial pretext, voted to suspend payment of clerical salaries and all financial support for religious activity. Five months later (3 Ventôse/21 February 1795) a more explicit decree was the logical culmination of public policy since the beginning of the Convention. The Republic now renounced all religious affiliation. While reiterating commitment to the religious freedom first proclaimed in 1789, it forbade any public sign or display of religious commitment. France was now to be a completely secular state. This decree was the origin of the principle of *laïcité* still pursued by the Fifth Republic.

* * *

BUT DISENGAGEMENT PROVED no solution. Its immediate consequence was a surge in overt religious practice. Easter 1795 saw a record turnout of worshippers as shops closed on Sunday in defiance of the republican calendar. Officiating were many priests released from detention as suspects, and although there were now not nearly enough, and many services took place without them, the fears that had prompted their imprisonment remained. The pope was still an enemy of the Republic, and nonjurors had refused oaths of loyalty on his instructions. Nor did most of these priests disguise their royalism, especially after June when, on the death of Louis XVI's surviving son in republican captivity, his exiled uncle proclaimed himself Louis XVIII in the Declaration of Verona, promising that when restored he would re-establish the Church in its former power and glory. The deputies of the Convention recognized that the rebel departments of the west had been calmed and apparently pacified by allowing priests to minister to their flocks undisturbed. But, as they began finalizing a new constitution containing renewed guarantees of freedom of religion, they could not contain their persistent suspicions. Thus a special decree of 29 September (7 Vendémiaire, Year III) imposed yet another oath on all 'ministers of religion'. They were required, on pain of fines or imprisonment, to recognize the sovereignty of the nation and to promise submission and obedience to the laws of the Republic. But over the next four years the Republic's laws on religious matters would fluctuate dramatically, making it virtually impossible for any priest to remain in good civic standing.

The very passage of this law reflected an atmosphere of alarm in the Convention as its end approached. Many deputies feared that elections to the legislative councils under the new constitution would produce counter-revolutionary majorities. And when they attempted to pre-empt any such results by stipulating that two-thirds of the new deputies should be chosen from among themselves, the reaction of thwarted royalists was to mount an insurrection in Paris, the uprising of 13 Vendémiaire, Year III, put down by troops and artillery under the command of General Bonaparte.

* * *

THIS WAS THE start of his public career, shooting down Catholic royalists. Not long afterwards he met the widow Beauharnais, and after a whirlwind romance they were married. Authentically republican, it was a civil ceremony, though with procedural flaws which came back to haunt the couple eight years later. It is also possible that the next day they went through a religious ceremony conducted by a nonjuror, as Napoleon's brother Joseph had two years earlier.[5] But if so, it happened in secret, and Napoleon and Joséphine only became married in the eyes of the Church in a ceremony of 1804 on the eve of the imperial coronation. Meanwhile, within days of the 1796 ceremony the bridegroom left for his command in Italy. Here for the first time he would come into direct contact with the entrenched power of the Catholic Church.

In the aftermath of the Vendémiaire uprising, the last days of the Convention and the first of the new constitutional regime of the Directory brought renewed severities against nonjuring priests who had emerged from hiding, or returned from emigration, after the Convention's declaration of religious disengagement. The draconian laws of 1792 and 1793 against priests refusing the 'liberty equality' oath were officially renewed, and nonjurors were explicitly excluded from an amnesty to celebrate the new constitution. Despite the accelerating pace of religious observance among the laity, and especially resourcefully devout women, local authorities were instructed to be inflexible. And, while nonjuring clergy faced fresh persecution, the remnants of constitutional oath-takers, no longer funded by the Republic, sought to reorganize themselves. Immediately after the Convention had voted to stop funding, a group of oath-taking bishops, led by Grégoire, began to plan for their church's independent existence under the traditional name of Gallican. They welcomed the Republic's disengagement from religion in February 1795 and, urging sworn priests everywhere to unite, were able to secure the use of the cathedral of Notre Dame. Untroubled by clerical oaths, they felt well placed, while nonjurors incurred renewed persecution, to recapture the loyalty of priestless believers. But their numbers were few; they were torn by doctrinal disputes and issues of hierarchical authority, and dogged by persistent official suspicion of all priestcraft. Rome, meanwhile, consistently repudiated them as schismatics, loyal to a state which spurned God.

But relations with Rome were transformed by Napoleon's spectacular victories in Italy. Wherever they went, his soldiers were particularly brutal towards the clergy and ruthlessly plundered and desecrated churches and monasteries. And their general was under clear instructions from the Directory to make war on the defenceless papal states. His priority, however, was to defeat the Austrians, and only when they were temporarily at bay in June 1796 did he invade papal territory and occupy Bologna. Bereft of allies who had made peace in the face of French victories, the pope at once sued for an armistice. It cost him a heavy indemnity in cash and works of art, and French occupation of his rich northern territories. But in return, Napoleon did not march on Rome and flouted directorial instructions to demand the expulsion of thousands of French émigré priests from papal realms. Pius VI sighed with relief: the papacy had survived. But a deputation sent by him to Paris to explore a comprehensive religious settlement found the Directory intransigent; when revitalized Austrian armies reappeared south of the Alps, the pope reneged on the armistice. Napoleon's response was to create the Cispadane Republic from the occupied papal territories; but, even after he defeated the renewed Austrian push at Rivoli, he still did not march on Rome. 'My aim', he had already confided to a French diplomat, 'is to be called the saviour rather than the destroyer of the Holy See.'[6] Now he told a trusted cardinal that, 'Whatever might happen, I beg you ... to assure His Holiness that he can remain at Rome without any sort of worry. As first minister of religion he will find, under this title, protection for himself and for the church.'[7] Yet the pope knew he was now at the French general's mercy, and he rapidly agreed to negotiate surrender. The result was the Treaty of Tolentino (1 Ventôse/18 February 1797), under which the papacy at last recognized the loss of Avignon, in addition to that of its northern provinces now reconstituted as a French sister republic. It was also obliged to pay an indemnity of 30 million francs. Thus weakened, Napoleon assured the Directory, the papal state must soon collapse. Yet it seems unlikely that he really believed this. In Italy he had learnt to recognize the entrenched power of religion, which he did not intend to affront by inflicting public humiliation on the aged pontiff. 'I did not speak of religion,' he pointedly told the directors, 'because it is evident that by persuasion and hope these people can be made to take steps which can then be truly useful for our internal tranquillity.'[8]

Back in France, internal tranquillity still seemed a long way off. But over the summer of 1796, in the aftermath of the Babeuf plot with its creed of atheistic communism, the anti-clerical severities of the Directory's early months were relaxed. As the popular revival of religious practice continued, some émigré priests were allowed to return, a blind eye was often turned to those who had refused the oath of liberty and equality of 1792, and in December many nonjurors were set free when the reactivated penal laws of the preceding autumn were repealed. The thwarted conservatives of Vendémiaire were now organizing for the elections of 1797, when half the former members of the Convention imposed on the legislative councils in 1795 would retire, and the votes of newly annexed Belgium, a bastion of traditional Catholicism, would count for the first time. Fears of an imminent refractory revival also concentrated the efforts of Grégoire and the Gallicans to establish their independent legitimacy. They planned a national council, which eventually convened in August 1797 in Notre Dame. And by then the expected conservative surge had taken control of the councils. Despite a requirement that electoral assemblies take an oath of hatred for both royalism and 'anarchy', the spring elections brought a royalist landslide.

It coincided with Napoleon's final defeat of the Austrians. The victorious general set about consolidating a new Cisalpine Republic in northern Italy, absorbing the short-lived Cispadane created from former papal territories. And initially it seems he welcomed the electoral results in France as opening the way to religious harmony. Noting that one of the first acts of the new legislature had been to initiate repeal of remaining penal laws against nonjuring priests, he urged the pope to issue a bull enjoining the latter to preach obedience to the government and constitution, as a preliminary to reconciling clerical divisions. This would open the way to 'lifting all obstacles and . . . bring the majority of the French people back to the principles of religion'.[9] These words prefigured a fundamental principle of what he would negotiate with another pope four years later; and Pius VI appeared ready to co-operate now. But by the time he received the news, Napoleon had grown alarmed that the new legislative majority might also repudiate his Italian achievements and undo the terms he had imposed. He began to hint to the Directory that soldiers could be dispatched to support any move they might make to preserve the republican constitution. To reinforce his point, he sent Augereau to Paris, where troops could be put under his command. But the directors were split, and while they bickered among themselves, the legislative majority continued to repeal revolutionary legislation. A final abrogation of all religious penal laws passed since 1792 came on 7 Fructidor/24 August; but on that very day the presidency of the Directory passed to Louis-Marie La Révellière-Lépeaux, a philosophical anti-clerical of long standing. He had always been keenest among the directors in urging Bonaparte to humiliate the pope, and over the preceding months he had given official encouragement to a new deistic cult calling itself Theophilanthropy. With the support of Augereau's troops, a week later (18–19 Fructidor) he and fellow directors Barras and Jean-François Reubell removed the other two from office and decreed the expulsion of 177 deputies from the councils.

* * *

THE COUP OF Fructidor marked the beginning of what immediately began to be called the 'Directorial Terror'. The number of victims would be nowhere near as spectacular as that of 1793–4, but as then the nonjuring clergy bore the brunt of republican severity. Many thousands of refractories had returned from exile or emerged from hiding during the period of widening religious freedom since the start of the year, often to ecstatic welcomes from spiritually starved parishioners. Now the decree of 7 Fructidor, which had seemed to fulfil all their hopes, was abruptly rescinded. All the laws penalizing refractories, all the oaths and declarations required of them, were reactivated. And now there were new sanctions. All priests were required to subscribe to the oath of hatred towards royalty and 'anarchy' imposed on electors and officials in the spring. Refusers would be subject to deportation to the inappropriately so-called 'dry guillotine' of Guiana, on the mosquito-infested coast of South America. Additionally, the Directory reserved to itself the power to deport any priest suspected of 'disturbing public tranquillity in the interior' – in effect, a new and more arbitrary version of the Law of Suspects which had underpinned the Terror. All priests were subject to these sanctions, and even some of Grégoire's Gallicans felt unable in Christian charity to take an oath explicitly pledging hatred. Their national council was allowed to run its course until November, but for all its republican loyalism, the Gallican Church was obliged by the Directory, with studied contempt, to share Church buildings in rotation with La Révellière-Lépeaux's favoured cult of Theophilanthropy. Akin in many ways to Robespierre's Cult of the Supreme Being, Theophilanthropy sought to harness the religious feelings of citizens to republican patriotism. Its adepts met for priestless worship on the *décadi*, the republican day of rest; and general observance of the republican calendar was now enforced with renewed zeal. But Theophilanthropy never caught on much beyond the educated elites of certain cities, and by the time its leading patron resigned from the Directory in June 1799 its pallid celebrations were in obvious decline. By then it had largely been superseded in official standing by the *culte décadaire*, reinforcing observance of the republican calendar with even less emphasis on God and more celebration of civic and philosophic virtues.

These policies were underpinned by the conviction that Catholic priestcraft was the Republic's most dangerous enemy. Yet the expansion of the Republic had swelled its ranks. The annexation of the Austrian Netherlands in 1795 had added one of Europe's most clericalized regions to its territory. The Austrians formally recognized their loss in the Peace of Campo Formio, concluded within weeks of the Fructidor coup. But even before the coup, the Directory had begun to bring these 'reunited departments' into revolutionary conformity by confiscating Church property and dissolving monasteries. After Campo Formio the Belgian clergy, now French citizens, were subjected to the renewed penal laws, including the oath of hatred. French clerics were by now used to oaths; but to impose them on newcomers was to repeat the polarizing mistakes of 1790 – and now the penalties for refusal were harsher. The first to suffer the consequences was the Cardinal Archbishop of Malines/Mechelen, who urged his clergy not to swear hatred of monarchy. He was deported across the Rhine. But most lower clergy followed his instructions, and they began to be rounded up for dispatch to Guiana. This persecution accelerated when, from September 1798, the Jourdan Law introduced conscription with no exceptions for Belgium, this time repeating the mistake that had triggered the Vendée uprising. It provoked a similar response: resistance in the name of religion. The Belgian uprising proved more ephemeral than the Vendée. But by the time it faded away early in 1799 it was squarely blamed, by the Directory, on unsworn priests, 'sacerdotal scoundrels' who were 'the cruellest enemies of France'. It was decided to deport around 8,000 of them, so denuding the new departments entirely of priestly subversives. But nothing like that number were caught. Thousands fled east and north across the frontiers; many went underground. In the end, scarcely five hundred found themselves transported to the west coast to await embarkation for the fatal shore. There they joined three hundred compatriots sentenced before the blanket deportation, and over 1,300 nonjurors from the rest of France. But a mere 256 eventually reached Guiana on the only one of three transports not intercepted at sea by the British. The rest remained imprisoned in makeshift quarters or rotting hulks. Already disproportionally unable to escape capture through age or infirmity, hundreds died there.

Meanwhile, in Rome, the pope himself was believed to be at death's door. If he died, Napoleon told his brother Joseph, who was now the Republic's ambassador to the Holy See, he should try to ensure that there was no successor. But the crisis passed; and, having consolidated his Italian conquests with the Peace, Napoleon now turned his attention to defeating the only enemy of France left in the field, Great Britain. Soon all his energies were taken up in preparing for his great expedition to Egypt and, during this time, Italian affairs slipped beyond his grasp. The arrival of rapacious commissioners in Rome to extract the indemnities conceded at Tolentino provoked a backlash which culminated in the murder of a French general. Thereupon the Directory, against his advice, ordered what Napoleon had always refused to undertake – a military occupation of the Holy City. The anti-clericalism of the French Army was now unrestrained by their former general's pragmatism, and the occupiers happily encouraged co-operative Italian Jacobins to proclaim a Roman Republic on the lines of the new sister republics further north. At the same time, Pius vi was arrested and bundled out of his capital, at last a prisoner of the godless Republic.

Increasingly ill, he remained in Italy, on Tuscan territory but under French control, and in no sense a free agent. And when, in the spring of 1799, a new hostile coalition brought Austrian troops back into action in Italy, he was hurriedly moved ever further north to keep him out of their hands. Eventually the only safe place to hold him seemed to be France itself, and late in April he was carried across the still-frozen Alpine passes to a final resting place in Valence. His small, faithful entourage was surprised to find his passage greeted by devout and respectful crowds, but his military captors were implacable in their contempt for 'the former pope'. He died in their custody on 30 August 1799 while Napoleon was on the sea between Egypt and France.

* * *

IN EGYPT, EVEN more than in Italy, Napoleon showed himself determined to respect the power of religion. To win over the Islamic clergy, he heaped extravagant praise on the Qur'an and the Prophet, promised conversions among his soldiers and boasted of persecuting the pope in Italy and his destruction of the crusading Knights of Malta. They responded by urging the faithful to respect French rule as ordained of God. This did not prevent a major anti-French revolt in Cairo, and the savagery with which it was put down probably did more than these pious exhortations to maintain French control. But Napoleon kept up his public displays of respect for Islam until days before his departure. And back in France, on his journey north, he stopped in Valence to confer with Pius VI's bereft companions, watching over their master's still unburied remains. Something should be done, he implied, but he could do nothing for the moment.

There was no religious dimension to the general's seizure of power in Brumaire; but he clearly recognized at once that the religious situation was the most pressing domestic problem facing his government. It was true that, even as the Directory's agents were manhandling the dying pope across Italy, anti-clerical fervour within France was easing. Local authorities, anxious not to stir up further civil unrest, were often slow to implement ferocious measures decreed from Paris; and by the spring of 1798 the Directory itself was moving to curb the neo-Jacobin zeal initially unleashed in Fructidor. And when in the coup of 30 Prairial, Year VII/18 June 1799 the legislative councils ejected La Révellière-Lépeaux and Merlin de Douai, the most zealous anti-clericals, from the Directory, the persecuting impulse lost momentum. Some priests, who had taken all the oaths, and even married, but been imprisoned nevertheless, began to be released from the western hulks. Former priests were now in charge of the Republic – Sieyès a director, Fouché (from July) as police minister, although ex-bishop Talleyrand resigned from the foreign ministry at the same moment to await events. French reverses over the summer, however, had led the British to encourage so-called chouan warlords in the Catholic and royalist west to renew their resistance, and on the very day that Napoleon arrived back in Paris a chouan army stormed and sacked Le Mans. There were other less successful attacks on urban centres of republicanism throughout October, but not until he was established in power and new institutions were launched could the first consul turn his attention to religious matters.

His old confidant Talleyrand was now recalled to the foreign ministry, and late in December he used his web of contacts to set up a secret meeting between the new ruler and chouan leaders in Paris. Here they were the first to learn that the first consul had no intention of paving the way for Louis xviii. But if they would lay down their arms, he promised to abrogate emergency laws against insurgents and émigrés and to exempt their districts from conscription. Above all, he promised to guarantee freedom of worship. 'I shall re-establish religion,' he declared, 'not for you, but for me ... it is necessary for the people, and I will re-establish it.'[10] The next day he was as good as his word, reaffirming in a decree that 'the laws concerning freedom of worship will be executed in the letter and the spirit' and annulling orders that religious buildings should be open only on the *décadi*.[11] He also issued a proclamation to the western departments promising them, among other things, full freedom of worship and use of religious buildings and urging the 'ministers of a God of peace' to preach reconciliation and concord in their re-opened 'temples'. By this time, too, he must have known that the papacy had not breathed its last with Pius vi.

On 30 November, by permission of the emperor, a conclave had opened in Venice to elect a successor. It was true that the only French influence there, the notoriously intransigent Cardinal Jean-Siffrein Maury, saw himself as representing Louis xviii; but the first consul sent a conciliatory signal by finally authorizing a funeral for Pius vi, and bowing to the insistence of the pope's last companions that it could not take place in the local cathedral, since it was in the hands of Gallican clergy. But now he could only wait for the results of the conclave.

It deliberated for almost four months, and the candidate who emerged victorious surprised everyone. A Benedictine monk by training, Luigi Barnaba Chiaramonti had been Cardinal Bishop of Imola since 1785. He owed his elevation to his predecessor, whose name he took as Pius vii. At Imola, from 1796, he had had to confront French invaders at first hand and accept their seizure of papal territory. But his approach was never openly to defy them. He urged his flock to obey their new masters; and by the time of the conclave, he was best known (and to some, notorious) for a pastoral letter of 1797 in which he declared that the Catholic religion was quite compatible with republican democracy and even commended the religiosity of Rousseau. This reputation was scarcely calculated to appeal to the Austrians who had allowed the conclave to take place, and they spent the months after his election obstructing the new pope's desire to return to Rome. But by the time they allowed him to make the journey, they were themselves being swept out of Italy by the return of the French.

While he waited for the result of the conclave, the first consul began to consult informally with his closest advisers about how he might achieve reconciliation with whoever might be elected. But his main preoccupation throughout the spring of 1800 was his forthcoming campaign in northern Italy. And he knew from previous experience there that the clergy must be reassured. Within days of his epic crossing of the Alps he summoned the clergy of Milan to a meeting at which, speaking in Italian, he declared himself a fervent Catholic, and determined that 'the Christian, Catholic and Roman religion shall be preserved in its entirety.'[12] No society, he said, could exist without morality, and there was no good morality without religion. France had seen the error of its ways, and now the Catholic religion was resuming its former glory there. Finally, 'as soon as I am able to confer with the new pope, I hope to have the happiness of removing every obstacle which still hinders complete reconciliation between France and the head of the church.' Two weeks later, returning victorious from the field of Marengo, he organized and attended a celebratory *Te Deum* in the great cathedral. Then, dashing back to Paris, he spent a night at Vercelli, where the bishop was Cardinal Carlo Giuseppe Martiniana, the last cardinal to have seen the former pope alive. He asked the cardinal to write to Rome with an offer to negotiate a new concordat.

Now at last he began to reveal his full ambitions for a religious settlement. He had offered, the cardinal reported to Rome, to help the pope recover his domains, and to abandon the schismatical Gallican Church. He had insisted that there could be no question of restoring the Church's lost lands but undertook to pay a salary to bishops. He also insisted, however, that all existing bishops must be deposed and replaced by nominees of the government, invested by the pope only with spiritual authority.

Pius VII had never expected much from the man who had humiliated his predecessor in the Treaty of Tolentino. He had announced his election to the pretender as Louis XVIII of France, but not to the first consul. And there was much in the latter's new proposals to disappoint him. Could the head of the Church bring himself to accept the loss of all its properties in France? Was it even possible to depose bishops enjoying the apostolic succession? Yet the proposals contained some calculated inducements. After Marengo, it seemed that only France had the power to restore the papal state. The offer to pay ecclesiastical salaries in France would solve an obvious problem. And although it was a power no pope had claimed before, if bishops were to be deposed, who else but the pope could credibly do it? Above all, a settlement would bring an open and guaranteed 'restoration of the altars' for the long-suffering French faithful, and Gallican schismatics would be forever sidelined. Burdened though he was, therefore, by the immediate complexities of restoring papal authority in the Holy City after an interregnum of sixteen months, Pius VII gave the news a tentative welcome. He and his new secretary of state, Cardinal Ercole Consalvi, moved at once to choose a negotiator. They settled on archbishop Giuseppe Spina, who, as the faithful confidant of Pius VI and guardian of his unburied remains, was known to Bonaparte from their encounter at Valence in October 1799. After a delay of several months, Spina was summoned to Paris.

The delay had left the papal curia in alarmed puzzlement. But Napoleon was using the summer to test likely reaction to his plans among the republican elites of Paris. All of them were, to one degree or another, steeped in the anti-clericalism born of a decade of priestly subversion and defiance. In many ways, Napoleon shared it. His insistence on the deposition of bishops reflected his conviction that 'fifty émigré bishops paid by England are the leaders today of the French clergy. Their influence must be destroyed.'[13] But unlike his critics, he recognized that only the pope could achieve this. Over the summer a government-controlled press was fed stories vaunting the achievements of religious toleration; while in front of a sceptical Council of State the first consul launched his oft-to-be-repeated mantra that he had won over Egypt by posing as a Muslim and would now restore religious harmony in France by flaunting his Catholicism. But, not content with these extravagant claims, he also sought up-to-date information on the religious state of the country beyond the capital. The reports he received from councillors of state sent out to gather it were almost unanimous. They spoke of a constitutional clergy thinly scattered and poorly supported by the laity – although as good republican administrators the respondents urged recognition of these priests' loyalty to successive regimes. But all recognized that nonjurors enjoyed much wider support, especially among women, children and the better-off. They saw most refractory clergy as subversives, unreconciled to the loss of the privileges and domination they had enjoyed under the monarchy. Yet few thought that sustained persecution would contain them or reduce their influence. Conciliation would be far more effective. Reports from Brittany and the west noted that when nonjurors were allowed to operate openly, taxes were paid and brigandage shrank away. Governments should learn, reported the councillor of state sent to Nantes, that 'if they do not have the priests for them, they will have them against. Ministers of religion are never indifferent in the march of empires; if the laws do not favour them, they work to overturn the laws and those who make them.'[14] The first consul could not have agreed more. 'How can there be order in a State without religion?' he exclaimed to Roederer.[15] 'Society cannot exist without unequal fortunes, and inequality of fortunes cannot exist without religion ... And so the government, if it is not master of the priests has everything to fear from them.'

Yet many of his Brumairian collaborators remained unconvinced. Even those who accepted that the separation of Church and State since 1795 had not worked thought that other solutions were preferable to reintroducing the authority of a 'foreign prince'. Some thought it would be better to follow the example of Henry VIII of England and establish a national Protestant Church. Later, to force the pope's hand, the first consul was prepared to threaten this, but he never really thought the idea was practical. Protestants were few in France, he observed, and the devout majority of Catholics would never wish to be identified with them. Other councillors, impressed by the dogged republican loyalty of the former constitutional clergy, urged him to restore their status as a national Gallican Church, independent of Rome. And throughout the early months of the consulate, Napoleon was in regular contact with their spokesman, Grégoire, whose opinions he always seems to have respected. Yet again, however, he knew how little popular support the Gallicans enjoyed, and he saw them largely as another bargaining counter to overcome papal obduracy.

Determined, therefore, to push on with his project, he welcomed Spina's discreet arrival in Paris in early November with a reassuring interview. Then the papal envoy was introduced to the other side's improbable negotiator, the Abbé Etienne Bernier. A native of the Vendée, Bernier had spent years with western insurgents fighting for Church and King. But after the disappointments of the last chouan uprising the previous winter, he finally recognized a lost cause, and rallied to France's new ruler. Behind him stood an even more notorious turncoat: Talleyrand, still technically a bishop though excommunicated by Pius vi as the instigator in 1789 of the confiscation of church lands, and the prelate who, two years later, had conferred the apostolic succession on the first constitutional bishops. Ever the diplomat, Talleyrand avoided direct contact with the papal envoy, who could be presumed to hold him in abhorrence. But at every stage, Bernier reported back to him for his well-qualified observations. Equally influential was François Cacault, a diplomat with experience of dealing with Rome going back to the campaigns of 1796 and 1797 and beyond. Initially Bernier reported rapid progress in negotiations with Spina, but the first draft of an agreement was torn to pieces by Talleyrand and Cacault. The papal envoy expected the Roman Catholic religion to be declared the religion of the nation and the state: the two diplomats declared that the state should have no religion, and tolerate all. Catholicism was merely the religion of the great majority. They thought the proposed terms of papal recognition for the loss of church lands too equivocal and brushed aside all doctrinal objections to the outright dismissal of bishops. They also insisted that constitutional priests, and the thousands among them who had married, should be treated less harshly by restored papal authority than Spina had proposed. The effect was to prolong negotiations far further than the first consul had been led to expect – much to his fury. And these frustrations were exacerbated by the fact that Spina had been authorized to sign nothing without referring back to Rome.

By the turn of the year, however, Spina's position had been weakened. Austria, the leading Catholic power, had been finally defeated at Hohenlinden and was now seriously negotiating peace. And on 24 December the first consul had survived the most serious attempt on his life so far. He was happy to blame it publicly on Jacobins but was soon convincingly informed by Fouché that it was the work of Catholic monarchists. He now began once more to cultivate Grégoire, and Spina was alarmed by a new suggestion that a restored bench of bishops might include a number of Gallicans. As peace was finally concluded with the Austrians in February 1801, Spina was presented with a new draft concordat, approved by the first consul in person, which ignored most of the papacy's earlier proposals, and was accompanied by the demand that he be given full authority to accept it without delay.

The response from Rome was silence, as congregations of cardinals picked over the proposed terms with deliberative disgust. In Paris, Napoleon, who wanted to promulgate a concordat at the same moment as the peace already signed with Austria, was frantic with frustration. He raged at Spina, demanding acceptance of the latest French terms within five days of their receipt in Rome. Otherwise he threatened to invade the papal states, and to declare an independent national church which might even be Protestant. Meanwhile, Cacault was sent to Rome as the Republic's ambassador. From there he urged patience, but his master in Paris kept up the pressure. He now authorized Grégoire and his Gallicans to convene a second national council, while Fouché ordered all authorities to treat 'insubordinate and fanatical' nonjuror priests with renewed severity. It appeared that the negotiations were on the brink of breakdown when Cacault, seemingly on his own initiative, suggested to the pope that he send a plenipotentiary to Paris with full authorization to agree terms. To emphasize this, a cardinal of the first importance was chosen: none other than the secretary of state, Consalvi. He arrived in Paris in the third week of June 1801 just days before the Gallican National Council convened in Notre Dame. Though widely known to be taking place, Spina's negotiations since the previous November had been conducted in discreet privacy. Consalvi's arrival was a public event, and he was urged to come to his reception by the first consul arrayed 'as much like a cardinal as possible'. The implication was that agreement was at last near.

Consalvi was indeed now prepared to concede much of what Spina had originally found unacceptable. But still there were sticking points. Napoleon demanded acceptance of his latest terms within five days – but it took over three further weeks, two more drafts and some frenzied last-minute bargaining before the cardinal was ready to sign an agreement on behalf of the pope. He had recognized, in the meantime, how unpopular the first consul's policy was, at least among the elites of the capital. 'The war which has been roused to prevent reunion with Rome', he reported early in July, 'is incredible. The whole body of magistrates, all the philosophes, all the libertines, a major part of the military, are against it.'[16] He knew, too, that Grégoire had opened the second national Gallican Council with a bitter attack on the papacy and its pretensions. In this light, Napoleon almost appeared as the Church's best friend, and certainly its best hope.

The seventeen clauses of the concordat signed on 15 July 1801 gave the papacy three main grounds for satisfaction. Above all, it restored the free and open exercise of the Roman Catholic religion in France after a decade in which it had never been secure and often persecuted. (Art. 1). Its unsold churches were restored to it (Art. 12), and the French government undertook to pay clerical salaries (Art. 14). Whatever his later quarrels with Emperor Napoleon, Pius VII never disguised his gratitude to the ruler whose determination had restored the altars. The Church's second great gain was not so immediately obvious, and the papal side had been reluctant to embrace it throughout much of the negotiations. It was agreed (Art. 3) that the pope should remove all those holding French bishoprics, by inviting them to resign or, in the event of refusal, stripping them of their powers regardless. No previous pope had ever claimed such comprehensive powers, and the pre-revolutionary Church would never have accepted them. Now they proved the springboard for a renewal of papal authority over the entire Church that would be the achievement of the nineteenth century. The third great gain reinforced this. The concordat embodied no recognition for the constitutional church or any claims to Catholic doctrine not authorized by Rome. Although the Gallican National Council continued to deliberate after the signature of the concordat, it came under immediate pressure from the government to wind up its proceedings. Fouché urged this course in honeyed words, but the determination was clear; and the council concluded on 16 August, the day after the pope in Rome had given his formal sanction to the concordat.

Not everybody in Rome was satisfied. Several cardinals urged rejection, or some renegotiation, on the grounds that the Church's losses far outweighed its gains. It had begun the negotiation asking to be recognized as the state religion, or at least the dominant one. All it got was to be acknowledged as the religion of 'the great majority of French citizens'. All clergy were to offer public prayers for the Republic and the consuls (Art. 8) and take an oath of obedience to and co-operation with the government (Art. 6). The Church had also hoped for the return of, or compensation for, the lands confiscated in 1789. Instead, it was forced to accept (Art. 13) that they were lost for ever. It had to agree to a complete redrawing of the ecclesiastical map (Art. 2), reducing the number of dioceses by more than half, and accept that, as before 1789, bishops should be nominated by the government and receive only their spiritual powers from Rome (Art. 4). In all this, Napoleon got what he had wanted from the very beginning. French religious life was now to be firmly in the government's hands; clergy accepting papal authority could scarcely any longer be actual or potential agents of the Bourbon pretender and holders of former church lands could at last enjoy the profits of the Revolution without fear of challenge.

Almost as important was what the concordat did not mention. Some matters arose repeatedly during the negotiations but were deemed too intractable for inclusion: should constitutional clergy be required to retract their oaths before reconciliation with Rome? Should clerics who had married be readmitted to the sacraments as laymen? A special papal brief was later secured to absolve former bishop Talleyrand, who promptly married his mistress. Nothing, meanwhile, was said about monks and nuns, whom Napoleon regarded as idle parasites. And although, in his original approach to Martiniana, he had hinted that he might help restore lost territories to the papal states, and Spina had been authorized to broach this question, the creator of the Cisalpine Republic, now renamed Italian, showed no interest in returning some of its richest parts to papal rule. An innocuous-sounding phrase in the concordat, finally, opened the way to further unilateral action, which was doubtless already in the first consul's mind: the public exercise of religion was to 'conform to rules of police that the government shall deem necessary for public tranquillity' (Art. 1).

Though ratified by the government as early as 10 September, the concordat was not formally proclaimed as a law of state until

Easter Day, 18 April 1802. Partly, this was because Napoleon hoped to issue it alongside the treaty with Great Britain, already under negotiation, finally bringing peace to all of Europe. Most of the delay, however, stemmed from difficulties in implementing the agreement. Brushing aside the doubts of his cardinals, Pius VII moved at once to remove bishops as agreed and sent Cardinal Giovanni-Battista Caprara to Paris as his legate. On the French side, Jean-Etienne-Marie Portalis, a returned émigré now a councillor of state, was placed in charge of all religious matters. But when Caprara demanded that all constitutional clergy retract the oath of 1790 before receiving papal recognition, Portalis, backed by Napoleon, refused. Oath-takers, they said, should not be compelled to renounce their original commitment to the Revolution. The first consul was determined to appoint a number of constitutionals to the new bench of bishops, and none elected as bishops since 1790, not even Grégoire, refused to resign. Nor did most of the nonjurors. Fifty-five obeyed, but 38 (all exiles) refused and were duly deposed. Meanwhile, under the constitution, the concordat could only become law when formally passed by the legislature, and those who hoped still to block it planned to do so at the scheduled session in November. Rumours were rife, but the press had been forbidden to raise religious questions, so there was no public discussion. The only hint of government commitment to religious restoration came when, on 4 October, the last relics of the cult of Theophilanthropy were closed down. Though now few in number, the first consul observed, in their anticlericalism these people behaved less like a religious sect than a club. The very word, evoking Jacobinism, was a condemnation.

Yet so worried was he about getting the concordat approved that it was not immediately presented. The Legislative Body, which at once made its intentions clear by electing a notorious anti-clerical as its president, had to content itself with sniping at other bills embodying peace treaties and sections of the new code of laws. Napoleon found this irritating enough, and a clear indication of what he might expect when the concordat was presented. It was this which prompted the first constitutional adjustment since Brumaire. All bills were withdrawn and, taking advantage of ambiguities in the wording of the constitution, the Senate was entrusted with renewing the personnel of both the Tribunate and the Legislative Body. It did not renew the mandates of members known to have opposed the government's bills, or who were likely to obstruct the concordat. They were replaced by candidates expected to be more docile. The chambers were then reconvened for a 'supplementary session', where the first bill to be presented embodied the long-awaited concordat.

It was not only likely legislative obstruction that had delayed its presentation, however. Lists of potential nominees to the new bench of bishops had been circulating since the previous spring, and the fear of the papal representatives had always been that they would include a number of constitutionals. These apprehensions were realized when, in March 1802, Caprara was presented with a list of sixty nominees, which included eleven of the dreaded schismatics. Napoleon regarded this as essential to his policy of religious reconciliation and was unmoved by the legate's protests. An even worse shock was to come. Portalis had used the delay in promulgating the concordat to draft the 'rules of police' mentioned in the first article. So that when the concordat was finally presented for legislative approval on 5 April it was accompanied by a detailed series of 'organic articles' previously unseen by the pope's representative. They comprised a detailed prescription of the future organization and powers of the Church in France. Their overall effect was to prevent any papal contact with the clergy without the government's permission. The word 'Gallican' was now used, as before 1789, to describe the whole French Church and not, as more recently, its constitutional variant; and the four Gallican Articles of 1682, formulated by Louis XIV in an earlier quarrel with

Rome to limit papal pretensions, were now to be taught in seminaries, even though subsequently renounced by Louis XIV himself. The prohibition of all 'ecclesiastical establishments' other than cathedral chapters and seminaries was an implicit rejection of monasticism. These provocations were scarcely compensated by the official re-establishment of Sunday as a day of rest and worship. Unwelcome, too, in Roman eyes, must have been another set of organic articles to regulate Protestant worship, a clear affirmation of the revolutionary principle of religious freedom and equality, even if both Lutheranism and Calvinism were subjected to the same detailed regulation and control as the Gallican Church. The first consul made it known that he expected the whole religious package to be passed unanimously. Even after the earlier purge, however, there were some votes against – but only a handful in either house. The whole process only took a few days. By now a final treaty between all belligerents in the war had been signed at Amiens, and both achievements were celebrated on Easter Sunday, 18 April 1802.

It was scarcely a coincidence that only four days earlier a new celebration of Christian beliefs was announced in the form of François-René de Chateaubriand's *Génie du christianisme*. Traumatized by news of his mother's death in 1798, the Breton wanderer had begun a work to expiate his youthful scepticism among the pious émigrés of London. Part of it had been printed there when the founding of the consulate offered the chance of returning to France. Here Chateaubriand was immediately taken under the patronage of the journalist Louis de Fontanes, a friend from his London days who was a protégé of the Bonaparte family. Soon achieving literary recognition for his romantic novelette, *Atala*, the suddenly fashionable author was encouraged by Fontanes to complete his unfinished eulogy of Christian faith as the negotiations with Rome progressed. Napoleon approved, and singled him out for public congratulation on his timely defence of religious truths.

Chateaubriand's honeymoon with France's new ruler would prove short, but for the moment the boost was mutual.

A lavish procession accompanied the consuls from the Tuileries Palace to Notre Dame, where they took communion at a solemn mass and heard a sermon from the newly appointed archbishop Boisgelin of Tours. A nonjuror, he was deliberately chosen as the priest who, as archbishop of Aix, had preached at the coronation of Louis XVI in 1775. Bells tolled, guns boomed, devout crowds applauded. But not everyone was happy. The many soldiers on duty, who had often spent years facing hostile populations inspired by what they remembered as fanatical priests, were visibly disgusted. General Moreau, the victor of Hohenlinden, ostentatiously stayed away. And when the first consul incautiously asked another general how he found the display, the reply was, 'A fine monkish mummery. All that was missing were the million men killed to stop what you've brought back.'[17] It was a decade before the battle-hardened General Delmas was employed again.

The reproach was taken personally because, not unjustifiably, Napoleon regarded the concordat as his personal achievement. He remembered it, on St Helena, as the most difficult thing he had ever succeeded in.[18] The religious divide was the oldest and deepest wound inflicted on France by the Revolution. Napoleon even once opined that if the revolutionaries had left religion alone, millions would scarcely have known there had been a Revolution.[19] This seems unlikely, but the commitment of most of the French population to religious belief throughout all the traumas of the 1790s was obvious enough. It was during his presentation of the signed concordat to a sceptical Council of State, which he had kept well away from the negotiations, that he made his famous remark that his aim was to govern as the majority wished to be governed. Nor did he underestimate the authority of the pope. 'I want to treat the pope', he told Spina, 'with as much regard as if he had four hundred thousand men.'[20] Unlike his closest counsellors, including those truculent former priests Talleyrand and Fouché, he recognized that only the pontiff could bring the nonjurors and their flocks to heel. 'I believe today,' he declared in 1818, 'as I believed in 1801, that the concordat was useful, necessary to religion, to the Republic, to the government. Churches were closed; priests were persecuted . . . émigré bishops were in the pay of England. The concordat put an end to these disorders; it brought the Catholic, apostolic and Roman church out of ruin.'[21] It also consolidated consular power in a way that nothing else could, by cutting the spiritual ground from beneath royalist counter-revolution. Church and King could no longer be allied against the Republic as they had been for a decade. Finally, and not least, papal recognition for the loss of the Church's former lands and properties reassured those who had bought them of the security of their gains. For them, more than anybody beside Napoleon himself, the Revolution had been triumphantly concluded. 'So why are you complaining about the concordat?' he allegedly asked the atheist intellectual Pierre Jean Georges Cabanis. 'It's a vaccine for religion.'[22]

It is true that harmony between rival clergy was not instantly re-established. The legate Caprara kept trying to induce constitutionals to renounce their past, and some recalcitrant bishops sought to pack their parish clergy with priests of their own persuasion. The first consul even had to remind his own uncle, Joseph Fesch, whom he had made archbishop of Lyon, that 'the Concordat ought not to be the triumph of any party, but the reconciliation of all.'[23] Nor would truly easy relations between France's ruler and the papacy ever be established. Conflict began at once over Napoleon's determination to introduce an Italian concordat, and it escalated on a range of issues over the next decade. By 1813 Pius vii, like his predecessor, was a prisoner in France, facing threats reminiscent of those thrown at Consalvi in 1802.[24] But the essence of the concordat was never in danger and survived its architect, because it gave most of the French what they wanted: a guaranteed right to practise their religion openly and in communion with the visible head of the Church.

Antoine-Jean Gros, *Napoleon Bonaparte as First Consul*,
1802, oil on canvas.

4

Restoring Authority

Congenitally insubordinate towards any power established above him, Napoleon as a trained army officer nevertheless believed that legitimate authority must have its due. He hated and feared disorder. In Paris, in the summer of 1792, he was a horrified eyewitness to the death throes of the Bourbon monarchy. As a mob of sansculottes burst into the Tuileries Palace on 20 June to intimidate the king into reinstating dismissed ministers, the young Corsican poured out his disgust to a passing acquaintance. If he were king, he said, such scenes would not happen. Nor did they, when he was. But he only became a hereditary monarch almost five years after he took charge of France's destiny and had still not taken the final step when his victorious peace came to an end in 1803. And although until then the language of republicanism was always on his lips, suspicion that monarchy was his ultimate aim was being voiced from the moment the Brumaire coup succeeded. Some of his closest associates in the coup, such as Roederer, were indeed hopeful from the start that he would make himself a king. They saw this as the only permanent solution to the problem of executive authority, which had dogged the entire Revolution.

Napoleon believed that the fate of what he always called the 'unfortunate' (*malheureux*) Louis XVI was unjust. He was 'guilty only of the crimes of others'.[1] And Napoleon was convinced that the Revolution had not been against monarchy when it began. 'The fall of the monarchy', he said to Chaptal, 'only followed from the difficulties put in its way. It was in no way the intention of

the revolutionaries.'[2] Nor was he wrong. Although the extrava-
gance of Queen Marie Antoinette – never popular, as a symbol of
a mistrusted Austrian alliance – attracted frequent hostile comment, Louis xvi was a well-respected ruler. His good heart and
benevolent intentions were repeatedly invoked in the cahiers of
1789, that first public opinion poll of modern times. It is true that
a few excited pamphleteers in 1789, such as Camille Desmoulins,
excoriated the depredations of monarchy throughout the history
of France and argued for a republic, but he offered no proposals for
how to reorganize executive authority.[3] And if most French people
on the eve of revolution had no thought of living without a king,
most clearly wanted to limit his power. The most regular aspiration expressed in the cahiers was for a constitution – to define and
circumscribe the government's authority while establishing some
form of national representation. The aim was to turn an absolute
monarchy into a constitutional one. This mandate was embraced
by the Estates-General despite all the procedural wrangling of its
first six weeks in May and June 1789. The revolutionary moment
came on 17 June, when the deputies of the Third Estate, supported
by a handful of parish clergy, proclaimed themselves the National
Assembly. The next day they cancelled, but promptly re-authorized,
all the taxes. It was a seizure of sovereign power in the name of
the French Nation. National sovereignty became the Revolution's
founding principle, and one which all subsequent regimes, including Napoleon's, acknowledged.

But if the nation was sovereign, where, from 1789 onwards, did
that leave the king? In the old absolute monarchy, the king as sovereign combined both executive and legislative power in his person.
The founding revolutionaries were determined that legislation
should now be the sole prerogative of the sovereign nation's elected
representatives. And although, after several days of frenzied debate,
it was later conceded that the king should be allowed a suspensory
veto on new laws he did not like, it could be overridden if two

succeeding legislatures insisted. It is true that executive authority would still be vested in the person of the monarch, with the freedom to appoint ministers; but the rest of the administrative hierarchy was to be elective. It is true, too, that the king was left in charge of foreign relations and command of the armed forces; but the result of the next international crisis to arise, six months into 1790, was to induce the Constituent Assembly to assign the final say on war, peace and international treaties to the legislature. The legislature was also empowered to fix the royal income in a civil list. Coinage might still bear the king's head, but a new civic oath pledged loyalty to the nation, the law and the king – in that symbolic order. Though still a monarch by hereditary right, Louis xvi was no longer styled king of France, but king of the French. The constitution even set out circumstances in which he might be deposed.

Initially the king was slow to realize how much authority he was losing. 'It's only a phase,' he reputedly said when told that the deputies had proclaimed themselves a National Assembly. But once the women of Paris had forced him, in October, to leave Versailles for the capital, he soon recognized that he was a prisoner with no force to rely on for protection or enforcement of his authority. Installed in the long-empty and scarcely furnished Tuileries Palace, he found himself stripped of most of the ceremonial trappings of the court of Versailles. He believed it dangerous and imprudent to oppose or attempt to veto any of the Constituent Assembly's decrees, and by the end of 1790 he was contemplating plans for escape. When these came to fruition in June 1791, before setting out on his ill-fated Flight to Varennes, he left behind an emotional denunciation of all he had undergone since the October Days. In the absence of any coercive power, he declared, government had become impossible.

The new rules, instead of bringing balm to wounds, are sharpening discontents instead; countless slanderous newspapers and pamphlets, simply echoing clubs, are sustaining disorder, and never has the assembly dared to remedy matters; the drift is only towards a metaphysical government, impossible to exercise.

However self-interested the former absolute monarch's lament for lost authority may have been, it was accurate enough. The constitution-makers of the National Assembly, mesmerized by what they remembered as the unchecked despotism of the pre-revolutionary monarchy, had reduced the king to a figurehead who could do hardly anything without the consent of an independent legislature where he had no direct influence. The initial response of the Assembly to the king's letter was defiant. All the restrictions that it had imposed on royal power, it claimed in a public address, had been justified now that the nation was sovereign. It also noted that government had gone calmly on even in the absence of the 'first public functionary'. On his ignominious return from Varennes he was suspended from office, and not restored until he accepted the completed constitution three months later. All this posed an implicit question. Did the nation now need a king for government to function?

Thousands of Parisians thought not. The king's flight unleashed a surge of popular republicanism. It culminated on 17 July when crowds of between 20,000 and 25,000 converged on the Champ de Mars to sign a petition against reinstatement of the disgraced monarch. National Guardsmen were sent to disperse them under martial law, resulting in the death of around fifty of the petitioners. The 'Massacre of the Champ de Mars' was followed by weeks of repression, which temporarily drove republicanism underground. But now it had its martyrs.

Despite their temporary suspension of the monarch, most members of the Constituent Assembly were terrified by his attempt to escape from the situation they had crafted for him. They could not imagine a stable constitution without a king, however constrained, as its keystone. Hiding behind the much-derided fiction that the Flight to Varennes had been a kidnap, they hurriedly finalized the constitution with a few cosmetic changes and virtually begged Louis xvi to accept it. Irrespective of all his previous denunciations, he did so. But by this time, other European monarchs, and swelling numbers of aristocratic émigrés, were openly talking of using force to restore him to his old powers; and in any case the indelible memory of Varennes had left him under constant suspicion. So that when he used his undoubted constitutional right to veto punitive laws passed by the new Legislative Assembly against émigrés and unsworn priests, the very act was widely perceived as counter-revolutionary. Over the winter months of 1791–2 an atmosphere of war fever was whipped up by radical deputies determined to expose the king as a traitor. Yet this scarcely disconcerted him. Witnessing the obvious decay in organization and discipline which had pervaded the army since 1789, he felt sure that it would be swept aside by the well-drilled conscript cohorts of German monarchs. So he offered no resistance to the Assembly's clamour for war against Austria in April 1792. He was convinced that the queen's nephew in Vienna would soon rescue them from constitutional constraints and put an end to the Revolution.

Initially his doubts about the army seemed justified, but the collapse of France's opening offensive did not have the results he hoped for. It merely intensified suspicions that the queen was leaking war plans to Vienna. And when the king refused once more to sanction repressive measures against nonjuring priests, it helped to produce the popular demonstrations which so disgusted Napoleon. Only seven weeks later, as unopposed Prussian and Austrian forces prepared to converge on Paris, threatening to sack the city if any harm came to the royal family, the appalled young officer was still in the capital to witness the storming of the Tuileries, the slaughter of the king's Swiss guards and the overthrow of the monarchy itself. 'On the tenth of August,' he later recalled, 'I felt that, if I had been called upon, I would have defended the king: I turned against those who founded the Republic through the people; and when I saw civilians attacking men in uniform, that shocked me.'[4]

France now entered upon its first experiment with republicanism, which Napoleon would terminate a dozen years later. Its success was mixed from the very beginning. A republic was not formally proclaimed until 21 September, when the first session of the newly elected constitutional Convention unanimously decreed the abolition of monarchy. Only the day before, the French Army had turned back an invading Prussian force at Valmy, heralding six months of victory and occupation of enemy territory for the new regime. In an atmosphere of republican euphoria, the Convention put the former king on trial for 'a multitude of crimes' aimed at establishing tyranny and destroying the liberty of the French people. It found him guilty, but the deputies were divided on the penalty he should pay. In the end, the decision to execute him passed by the narrowest of margins, and was much influenced by fear of what the militants of Paris would do if he was reprieved in any way. For the Convention had met, and the Republic been established, in the shadow of the Paris prison massacres of early September. The Republic had been born, whether on 10 August or the early days of September, in bloodshed which the nation's elected representatives had been powerless to stop. The entire Convention felt shocked and ashamed, but most deputies recognized that there was no alternative to appeasing the capital's 'blood drinkers'. Those who did not, and said so – the Girondins – paid the price in June 1793 when militant crowds surrounded the Convention demanding their expulsion.

Among the accusations levelled at them when they faced trial later in the year was that they were crypto-royalists. Although the Convention's guilty verdict on Louis xvi had been almost unanimous, the subsequent debates on sentencing had revealed plenty

of residual reverence among many deputies for the fallen monarch. It reflected widespread dismay across the nation at his
overthrow. And within weeks of his execution in January, an overtly
royalist rebellion had broken out in the Vendée. Meanwhile, the
execution had brought the monarchies of Russia, Spain and Great
Britain into war against the Republic, with war aims no less than
the restoration of Louis xvi's heirs to the throne. Renewed defeats
for French arms over the spring in Belgium and Germany seemed
to make that prospect a real possibility. Then, after the sansculottes
had forced the Convention to purge the Girondins, a number of
major provincial cities defied its authority in the so-called 'federalist' revolt. Their motivation was more anti-Parisian than royalist,
but sincere royalists were undoubtedly involved. The rebels whom
Captain Bonaparte helped to defeat at Toulon in December 1793
had actually proclaimed the dead king's captive son, Louis xvii.
All this showed that the difficulty of fitting monarchy into a sovereign nation had not been solved by proclaiming a republic and
killing the king. Millions of French citizens, all of whom had
grown up as subjects of a divinely ordained hereditary ruler, still
believed that the nation needed a crowned head to focus its loyalty and embody its historic character. So, far from uniting the
nation by removing the last great vestige of the old regime, the
overthrow of monarchy had opened up a new source of division,
which soon enough would intertwine with the religious polariza-
tion already well established.

When news of the fall of Toulon to the British in the last days
of August reached Paris, it brought the sansculottes back into the
streets to intimidate the Convention. They demanded that the
Republic's enemies be confronted by making terror the order of
the day. In fact, the emergencies of the preceding six months had
already led the Convention down the path towards rule by terror.
A new republican constitution, hurriedly drafted in the weeks following the purge of the Girondins, had been suspended as soon

as it was published, and on 10 October the government of the Republic was proclaimed 'revolutionary until the peace'. Executive power was now vested in two committees of deputies, with the authority to override, in the name of the endangered Republic, all the restraints and safeguards proclaimed only four years earlier as the rights of all citizens. And so, only a year after its foundation, the French Republic embarked on a regime of fear and intimidation, which cost the lives, over less than a further year, of tens of thousands of its citizens. By these means, it survived the trauma of its birth but sullied its reputation for ever. 'The blood of victims', Napoleon later observed, 'puts down no roots, it kills them. It was terror that killed the Republic.'[5]

Many of its victims were certainly royalists. So were many of the imprisoned suspects released in the weeks after the fall of Robespierre and the end of government by terror in Thermidor of the Year II. In the backlash against bloodthirsty Jacobinism over the next year, widespread popular royalism resurfaced. The relaxation of terroristic restrictions on newspaper publishing unleashed a strident conservative press. Well-heeled street gangs harassed known Parisian Jacobins as 'terrorists', while across wide swathes of the south a 'White Terror' brought the murder of many who had wielded local power only months earlier. Despite its indelible tincture of monarchist nostalgia, open religious observance was once more allowed; and growing numbers of émigrés were running the risk of returning. The near-famine conditions brought on by the severe winter of 1795 also fanned royalist sentiments. When kings had ruled, many said, they had cared for their subjects' welfare far more effectively than the Republic for its citizens. Jacobin loyalists could counter that bread had also been more plentiful under the controlled economy of the Terror, and called for the activation of the suspended constitution of 1793, with its extensive commitment to social and economic welfare. This was the demand of the sansculotte insurgents who invaded the

Convention in Germinal (1–2 April 1795) and again in Prairial (20–23 May). But this time the deputies were not coerced. For the first time, a revolutionary legislature turned to regular troops for its protection. And there was no prospect of activating what was now deemed a 'constitution of anarchy' that had been 'dictated by tyranny and accepted by fear'. A whole new constitution was now being devised, offering a convenient opportunity to reinstitute some sort of monarchical executive. After all, the son of Louis XVI was still alive, a child in national custody. Might he not be educated up to the role of a responsible constitutional ruler?

But on 8 June 1795 'Louis XVII' died. Before the month was out, his uncle, the Comte de Provence, from exile in Verona, had declared himself Louis XVIII. In a public proclamation, he warned that when restored to the throne he would reverse everything that the revolutionaries had done since June 1789. At this very moment, meanwhile, a British-backed force of émigrés landed at Quiberon in Brittany to link up with royalist chouan guerrillas. By the time news of the Declaration of Verona arrived, the expedition was well on the way to defeat by the republican troops of General Hoche, but all this made any idea of compromise with monarchy, much less the House of Bourbon, unthinkable. So the constitution, finally produced by the Convention in August 1795, was resolutely republican. Executive power was invested in a directory of five men chosen by a bicameral legislature, renewable through one of their number retiring each year by lot. Members of the two houses, called councils, would be chosen by annual elections, on a franchise restricted to substantial property owners. The idea of a rich electorate reassured monarchists: a majority might yet be returned in favour of a king. But the Convention, well aware of this danger, decided to underwrite the constitution's first years by decreeing that two-thirds of its own members should sit in the new legislature. Royalists were outraged, and on 5 October they launched an insurrection to force the Convention to withdraw the Two-Thirds Law before the new

constitution came into force. It was the defeat of this Parisian uprising of 13 Vendémiaire, by troops under the command of General
Bonaparte, that first brought his name to national prominence.

Ever since his service at Toulon, under the patronage of
Robespierre's brother, he had enjoyed a Jacobinical reputation. On
the strength of this, he was appointed in the spring of 1795 to a
command policing royalist rebels in the Vendée. But, as the pop-
ulism of the early Revolution burnt itself out in the thwarted
uprisings of Germinal and Prairial, the young general's thoughts
and ambitions were now turning merely to the hope that the new
constitution would produce a 'firm and better organized government'.[6] And Victorine de Chastenay, whom he met on the way to
his new posting, reminisced years later that he seemed to have 'no
republican maxim or faith. I was surprised, but he was completely
open in this respect. He spoke to me of such resistance as the revolutionary movement had encountered, and averred that it was
too incoherent for any success to have been possible.' She concluded that he was keeping his options open: 'This young soldier
then had a fortune to found; he was still an adventurer.'[7] His career
gambles over the next four months certainly worked well for him,
catapulting him first to his Vendémiaire assignment, then to command of the Army of the Interior and finally the Army of Italy.

Although a defeat for royalist hopes, Vendémiaire reinforced
a lesson that counter-revolutionaries had begun to absorb earlier
in the spring from the suppression of the Germinal and Prairial
uprisings. The army was now a force in revolutionary politics.
And, as Bonaparte also explained to Mme de Chastenay, it had no
ambitions of its own:

> The mass of the armies was totally detached from the
> bloody events that unhappy France had been the scene of; it
> knew almost nothing about them, and he seemed to think
> that the army, constantly in the hands of whoever was in

power, would not influence party opinions, and would not take on any colour under a single direction.

Events would bear this out. The troops who had saved the Convention from the insurgents in Prairial were commanded by General Jean-Charles Pichegru, who had earlier led the successful invasion of the Dutch Republic. Royalists now began to speculate that if such a commander could be won over with his troops to the royalist cause, elections might not be the only route to a Bourbon restoration. Accordingly, over the summer, royalist agents began to sound him out. He was not unreceptive but, after a series of defeats over the winter, he resigned from the army. The search for another general willing to overthrow the Republic now focused on the new and startlingly successful commander in Italy.

The Directory, like the Thermidorean Convention before it, sought to combat the extremes of Jacobinism (or what it, and Napoleon afterwards, called 'anarchy') and royalism by seesawing between them. The consistent aim of successive directors was a moderate republic supported by secure property owners. Neither Jacobins, with their record of confiscations, forced loans and terror, nor royalists, with their exiled king committed to returning confiscated and alienated national lands to their former ecclesiastical and noble owners, could be trusted to take power, even through the regular annual elections that were the supposed bedrock of the constitution. During the new regime's first months, Jacobinism came back into favour in order to consolidate the defeat of royalism in Vendémiaire. But this leftward swing only facilitated the egalitarian conspiracy of Babeuf by the spring of 1796, and in the aftermath of that plot's discovery the forces of royalism were once more unmuzzled. The right-wing press, always better funded than radical journalism, was allowed to publish unhindered. Metropolitan conservatism, increasingly permeated by monarchists of varying stripes, found a meeting-point in the so-called Club de Clichy;

while beyond the capital a loose network of 'philanthropic institutes' spent months preparing for the first scheduled elections under the new constitution in the spring of 1797. Everybody knew that the built-in majority of former members of the regicide Convention could then be ousted. The directors were well aware of these preparations but, divided among themselves, they found few effective means of thwarting them. An oath of hatred both for 'anarchy' and royalism, imposed on all voters, proved completely ineffective. And so the legislative elections of 1797 were the freest, with the highest rates of participation, since 1791. They produced a landslide of support for a negotiated peace with the Republic's monarchist enemies, and the election of many deputies committed to 'not five rulers, just one'.[8] Pichegru now re-emerged as an elected deputy and was chosen to preside at the lower Council of Five Hundred. And although there could be no move immediately towards a royal restoration, the new deputies acted at once to bolster the hopes of its most reliable supporters by removing restrictions on the nonjuring clergy. Their calls for peace, however, loudly abetted by the conservative press, alarmed the armies that their gains in the field might be negotiated away. Bonaparte in Italy, fresh from imposing the preliminaries of Leoben on the Austrians, had discovered evidence of Pichegru's earlier royalist contacts and sent full details to the Directory. He warned his soldiers they might need to cross the mountains 'with the speed of eagles' to defend the Republic and the constitution against royalist machinations. 'You can save the Republic,' he wrote to the directors, and 'if you need force, call on the armies.'[9] 'What is the use of the victories we achieve daily?' he asked.[10] 'Internal plots are spoiling everything and make the blood we shed for the country useless.' These pleas for directorial action were scarcely an expression of confidence in the government. Months earlier, the general had already privately revealed his contempt for the politicians of Paris and his hopes of brushing them aside.[11] Now, writing to introduce himself to Talleyrand, newly returned from emigration to become foreign minister, he opined that the Revolution was not over, because nothing had been constructed on the ground it had cleared.[12] Were he in power, he hinted, the former bishop would be properly rewarded for all his services to the Revolution.

The immediate priority, however, was to stem the royalist tide. Assured that three out of the five directors were prepared to act against the new legislative majority, Napoleon sent Augereau from Italy to command troops who would abet them. The result was the purge of Fructidor, which removed two directors, ultimately 177 deputies including Pichegru, and closed down 42 newspapers. Thus the representative constitution of 1795 had failed its very first test; and Fructidor made clear that royalism would never be allowed to triumph through elections. Briefly, under the impact of directorial crackdowns on the press, on nonjuring priests, on former nobles and returned émigrés, all forms of royalism went to ground. But by the end of 1798, as a revived foreign coalition came together to reignite the war, a new strategy began to emerge. With an electoral path to power now closed, partisans of the Bourbons dreamed more than ever of a military coup, but secret attempts to win over the hero of Italy, though not explicitly rejected, evoked no response. So they also began to plan insurrections. Supported by British subsidies channelled through a co-ordinating 'Swabian agency', the philanthropic institutes re-emerged as counter-revolutionary cells throughout the south and west, plotting a network of uprisings to coincide with invasions by Austrian and Russian armies. On paper they numbered thousands of members. But truly committed activists were far fewer except in a handful of localities, and their attempts to co-ordinate their action, whether in time or organization, were chaotic. By the time they were ready to move in the summer of 1799, the Republic remained uninvaded as the enemy coalition began to fall apart. A planned attempt to seize the city of Toulouse in August chose as its target, of all places, one of Jacobinism's firmest urban strongholds and was repulsed after a few days. Sporadic disorder continued for several weeks across the southwest, during which several thousand rebels were killed or captured; but by the time Napoleon returned from Egypt, there was no more danger from southern royalists.

Yet even as he landed and made his way north, unrest flared up afresh in the traditionally royalist strongholds of the west. Aware of how fragile public order had always been there, the Directory had exempted nine western departments from the Jourdan Law on universal conscription voted in September 1798. But the exemption was explicitly temporary, and as the military reverses of the following spring brought the new law into full force, rumours spread that it could not last. These fears fuelled recruitment into a planned royalist uprising. So did widespread resentment at the Law of Hostages passed by the councils on 12 July, which empowered authorities in disturbed areas to imprison relatives of émigrés or rebels and confiscate their goods. Although too late to coalesce, as originally intended, with the now-defeated southern insurrections, and no longer able to count on collateral support from the faltering forces of the coalition, a gathering of royalist chiefs decided in mid-September to rise regardless. Five days after Napoleon landed, 3,000 chouans swept into Le Mans and sacked the city. Several Breton towns were also briefly attacked, and by the end of the month, much of Brittany appeared to be in rebel hands. The Republic's oldest problem, western support for Church and King, seemed as persistent and intractable as ever.

* * *

NEVERTHELESS, ALL ROYALISTS were disconcerted by the general who had now seized power in Paris. Did he intend at last to use his power to bring in the king? Louis XVIII himself hoped so. As soon as it became clear that the general had secured a firm grip on power, he wrote to him, urging him not to 'prefer a vain celebrity' to the glory of restoring France's legitimate monarch.[13] But the first consul had already made it clear to the leaders of the western rebels that he was no General Monck. When some of the chouans negotiated a truce at the end of November 1799, Napoleon seized the opportunity to bring two of their leaders to Paris under safe conduct. He met them on 26 December, promising religious flexibility to those who would pledge loyalty to his new regime. But he had not, he declared, taken power to restore the Bourbons. Two days later he published an open letter to the western departments, urging them to abandon the Bourbons – 'two men who have honoured neither their rank by virtue nor their misfortunes by deeds' – and rally to a new government which had already abrogated unjust emergency laws enacted the previous summer and rededicated itself to the defence of religious freedom. But 'if, despite all the measures taken by the Government, there are still men who dare to provoke civil war, the first magistrates will have only one sad, but necessary duty to perform, that of subjugating them by force.'[14] As soon as the truce expired in January he made good the threat. A fierce military onslaught was launched against the most notorious centres of *chouannerie* in which hundreds were killed. The western insurgency rapidly collapsed.

Yet the fundamental problem that Sieyès and his fellow conspirators had hoped to solve with a general's help, remained. The Republic (they thought) needed a much stronger and more securely based executive government than the Directory. At the beginning of 1795 that clear-eyed Swiss observer of the French scene, Jacques Mallet du Pan, had warned the emperor, Francis II, that although most of the French would never accept the return of the intransigent Bourbons, only about a quarter of them were firm republicans.[15]

The nation, taken as a whole, no longer has any political will: its fanaticism is dead; no formal political opinion now rules, neither Monarchy nor Republic is upheld; but everybody aspires to establish a stable government, no matter what, that will end the Revolution. There is no uniform view on the nature of this government: the secret and most general wish is certainly favourable to monarchy, but limited monarchy, and undecided on who the monarch should be.

After four years of directorial rule only maintained by repeated violations of the constitution, little of this had changed. And if the new ruler of France, with not a drop of royal blood, had serious monarchical ambitions, he took care to conceal them; as when, during the drafting of the new constitution, he spurned the idea of becoming a 'grand elector', insisting that all he wanted was a strong Republic.[16] He was content for the moment to enjoy the virtual powers of a monarch during his ten-year term as first consul.

But when, in the spring of 1800, he took to the field for the first time as head of state, he began to ponder what might happen if he were killed. The closeness of victory at Marengo increased his concern. 'The French', he told Roederer, 'can only be governed by me . . . I am persuaded that nobody other than me, whether a Louis XVIII or a Louis XIV, could govern France at this moment.'[17] He emphasized this conviction by replying at last to Louis XVI-II's letter of February. 'I have received, Sir, your letter,' he wrote on 7 September, 'I thank you for the decent things you say. You must not hope to return to France; you would have to walk over 100,000 corpses . . . Give up your interest to the ease and happiness of France. History will reward you for it. I am not insensitive to your family's misfortunes . . . I shall contribute with pleasure to the comfort and tranquillity of your retirement.'[18] Yet he had no natural successor. He had no children, professed not to want any and confessed that his greatest fear was that if he were killed at Marengo, one of his brothers might succeed him. Together he and Roederer reviewed the possibilities – names and modes of appointment. None appealed, and it solved nothing for Napoleon to declare that his 'natural heir was the French people'. Yet if death in battle was, for the moment, no longer likely, the consular life was now increasingly in danger from assassination plots. Royalists were dreaming up schemes as early as the spring of 1800.

Marengo aborted these plans. In any case, Fouché at the police ministry knew all about them. But the months after the pivotal battle engendered several fresh plots, both Jacobin and royalist. A Jacobin conspiracy to shoot the 'tyrant' at an operatic performance was followed by Fouché's agents from the start and publicly thwarted to inspire general thanksgiving. Weeks later, other republican malcontents constructed an 'infernal machine', a barrel full of explosives designed to blow up the first consul as he journeyed to his favourite rural retreat at Malmaison. Once again, Fouché's agents uncovered the plot, and the device under construction, this time with less publicity. But it seems to have given the idea of a roadside bomb to royalist conspirators, who, in December 1800, constructed one to destroy the hated usurper on his way to a concert. It missed him by seconds, but the huge explosion killed a number of bystanders and completely destroyed a range of houses. The noise was heard all over Paris. Affecting unconcern in public at the narrowness of his survival, in private Napoleon raged at the policing failures that had allowed the attack to happen. He ordered Fouché to round up all Jacobin activists and perennial suspects. The minister had to obey, although warning the first consul that the true culprits were not dissident republicans but royalists. Within days he was able to prove it, but by then all the last serious former terrorists and social radicals were in custody, facing deportation and, in the most serious cases, the death penalty – not for organizing this most recent and spectacular attempt on Napoleon's life, but (as he put it) 'for all they have done and all they still might do'. Fouché, meanwhile, soon identified the real royalist perpetrators, and although a number escaped capture, the most prominent were tried and executed.

Failure though it was, the whole episode underlined once more how much depended on one man's life. Nobody felt this more keenly than members of the first consul's numerous family, so suddenly pitched to prominence by his success. The most impulsive was Lucien Bonaparte, who had done so much to save the day for his brother in Brumaire, and was now reaping his reward as minister of the interior. In October 1800, amid the welter of assassination plots, he commissioned an anonymous pamphlet hinting heavily that the first consul should be made a hereditary monarch. Drawing a 'Parallel between Caesar, Cromwell, Monck and Bonaparte', it argued that, despite superficial resemblances, France's new ruler had nothing in common with Cromwell or Monck, but much to echo Caesar, a soldier of superior, providential abilities to whom his grateful fellow citizens had offered a crown. If Bonaparte should disappear without a designated heir, it warned, France would be plunged into civil war between 'the supporters of a degenerate race', discredited 'assemblies' or a succession of ambitious generals. Napoleon himself had possibly authorized the pamphlet's appearance, but he rapidly distanced himself when it produced a widespread republican outcry, especially among groups who had helped him to power – the army and the motley ranks of the 'Brumairians'. Fouché, already at odds with Lucien, pointed out to Napoleon that the pamphlet's vaunting of a general murdered for his ambition was a positive incitement to pre-emptive assassination. After a bitter face-to-face clash between the two rivals in the first consul's presence, Lucien angrily resigned and Fouché made a public bonfire of all the copies of the pamphlet that he could find. Lucien's face was saved by a rapid appointment as ambassador to Spain.

This fiasco only served to reinforce Napoleon's ever-growing obsession with controlling public opinion. Like most of his contemporaries, he believed that the Revolution had been brought about by irresponsible and uncontrolled scribblers. Thus he never doubted the power of the press. The Revolution's founding manifesto, the Declaration of the Rights of Man and the Citizen, had proclaimed a commitment to freedom of thought and expression, but it acknowledged that the law might prescribe some limits. Successive revolutionary regimes had not hesitated to set such limits, muzzling or unleashing controls on the press and publishing according to changing priorities. The last great crackdown, aimed at the always better-funded right-wing press, had come in the aftermath of the Fructidor coup. Many titles were suppressed, and attempts made to arrest and deport leading printers and journalists considered hostile to directorial policies. Further measures to control the press came just days before 18 Brumaire in the form of a restricted list of authorized titles. The consular constitution had nothing to say about the press, or any sort of freedom, but only weeks after its proclamation the same policy was adopted. By the decree of 27 Nivôse, Year VIII/17 January 1800 only thirteen Parisian titles were authorized to continue publication, and then only if they refrained from impugning 'the social pact, sovereignty of the people, the glory of the armies' and offered no 'invectives against the government and nations friendly or allied to the Republic, even when the articles are copied from foreign periodicals'. Within a few months three even of the authorized titles were suppressed for infringing these regulations, and the press was placed under the supervision of Fouché's police ministry. Periodically, from now on, the first consul himself would dictate thinly anonymous articles in the government's official *Moniteur*, vaunting his own achievements.

Although the great explosion barely a month later reinforced the pamphlet's warning, it was clear that the elites who underpinned consular power were not yet ready to see their man become a monarch. So for the moment he needed to proceed incrementally. Already, however, in February 1800 he had moved the seat of power from the Luxembourg Palace to the former royal residence at the Tuileries. Under the previous regime, all five directors had been based in the Luxembourg, but now the second and third consuls were assigned no quarters in the Tuileries. Prior to his ceremonial progress to the restored seat of government in a recommissioned royal coach, Napoleon ordered the felling of two Trees of Liberty planted in the forecourt and the painting out of revolutionary symbols within. Over subsequent months a whole series of protocols and routines, reminiscent of monarchical practice, were introduced – including regular receptions for foreign ambassadors and ceremonial public audiences. There were also increasing numbers of lavish military parades, always culminating in the appearance of the commander-in-chief, marked out by the modesty of a mere colonel's uniform. But Napoleon knew that the best way now to pursue monarchical ambition was to continue to appear effortlessly successful. Ever since the summer of 1800 two crucial sets of negotiations had been under way – with the Austrians, and with the pope. Both had been slow and difficult. But the Austrian logjam had been broken by Moreau's victory at Hohenlinden on 3 December, followed by an armistice agreed the very day after the failure of the royalist assassination plot. Within two months the Austrians had signed the Peace of Lunéville, a virtual capitulation to French demands, which brought the long-desired peace on the continent. It was true that Moreau at Hohenlinden had done more than the first consul at Marengo to bring about this triumph; but the peace was a virtual confirmation of Napoleon's own earlier achievements at Leoben and Campo Formio, and he kept his congratulations to Moreau to a bare minimum. News arriving at the same time from London of the resignation of Pitt aroused hopes of a final peace with Great Britain too; and, indeed, the new British government began to put out feelers within weeks. Negotiations with the papacy, however, were not going so well. They were, in fact, close to breakdown, and the curia seemed unimpressed by Napoleon's impatient threats. He wanted to proclaim peace with the emperor and the pope together, but this did not happen. Increasingly public talks with Rome did finally proceed, but a concordat was not concluded until July, and even then, implementation procedures were not agreed until the following spring. By then, peace preliminaries had also been agreed with Great Britain, and it was the final Peace of Amiens, rather than that of Lunéville, which was celebrated and proclaimed alongside the concordat at Easter 1802.

All these agreements, loudly trumpeted by a press reduced to a handful of government mouthpieces, cut the ground from under the royalist cause of the Bourbons. They deprived it both of spiritual support and the backing of foreign powers. It was also rapidly losing its most visible supporters as émigrés flocked to return to their native soil. They had begun creeping back into the country almost as soon as the Terror ended, but the periodic leftward swings of directorial politics had always made their position precarious. They had been under particular suspicion since the anti-royalist coup of Fructidor. Listed émigrés had to prove, with copious attestations from witnesses, that even if absent from home they had never left the country. They were still excluded from public office. And during the renewed emergency of the spring and summer of 1799, in 'disturbed districts' relatives of listed émigrés faced imprisonment as hostages for their area's good behaviour, and confiscation of property. These difficulties were easing somewhat by the time Napoleon returned from Egypt, but clearly he regarded the question of the émigrés as one of the most serious he would face. It was the very first one he raised when, the day after his return, he began to lobby the men whose support he knew he would need.

And almost the first executive action of the interim government after he seized power was to abrogate the Law of Hostages. The general went in person to announce their liberation to a group held in Paris. He condemned the injustice of the law in his appeal to western rebels late in December. It was true that the new constitution reaffirmed all laws against émigrés, declaring that their confiscated property was lost for ever. Republicans and buyers of those properties no doubt felt reassured. But on 2 March 1800 a list of exceptions to many anti-émigré laws was issued, and the next day the official lists of émigrés were closed. Exiles now began to pour back across the frontiers, and after Marengo the flow redoubled. Returners had to be registered, often using by now well-worn subterfuges, including extensive bribery of officials. By the autumn of 1800 Fouché, whose ministry had the rapidly expanding responsibility for policing the inflow, was pressing Napoleon for more comprehensive action. He got it on 4 October, when at a stroke, 45,000 names were removed from the lists on the sole condition that they took an oath of loyalty to the constitution. This did not mean that they escaped further police surveillance, as they doubtless understood. But Fouché wished to go further. He argued for a general amnesty for all but a handful of the Bourbons' closest supporters. The first consul was reluctant to go that far so long as the Republic remained at war. Advised by the lawyerly second consul, even then he favoured a commission to review applications to return on a case-by-case basis. Fouché, however, argued that those admitted by such a tribunal might then lay claim to the return of confiscated properties, having been absolved from the crime of emigration. An amnesty, on the other hand, was a pardon, not an acquittal, and left the penalty unchallengeable. Eventually, Napoleon was persuaded and, to coincide with the celebration of peace with the Church and all the powers of Europe, on 26 April 1802 a general amnesty was proclaimed for all émigrés, with the exception of 3,373 named individuals. These were men known by their record as committed to the Bourbon cause and too dangerous to be allowed to return, even if they wanted to. The rest were invited to do so, subject again to an oath of loyalty and a promise not to challenge the land settlement. And those whose former properties had not been sold were able, subject to certain restrictions, to reclaim them. Not everybody who took advantage of the amnesty returned reconciled to the new regime. Some saw it as an opportunity to work for a Bourbon restoration from within the country rather than abroad. The arrogance of other returners attracted widespread disapproval. But by absolving those who had left the country rather than live with the Revolution, and allowing them to return safely home, Napoleon's new regime neutralized thousands of potential opponents and turned some at least into grateful supporters. Almost by definition, few émigrés had been republicans. They were, therefore, unlikely to resist the regime's relentless progress towards monarchy.

The triumphant scenes at Easter 1802 appeared a perfect moment for accelerating the push. 'Nothing yet indicated', Cambacérès reminisced, 'that royalty might arise again in France, or that [Napoleon] had the intention of forming a fourth dynasty.'[19] 'I have made kings,' he said to Joséphine as 1802 began, 'with no wish to be one.'[20] Nevertheless, Cambacérès noticed that 'without being less accessible, he demanded more respect from those who approached him. It was noted above all that he made a point of exalting several institutions that had been destroyed, and deprecating others which owed their birth to the Revolution.'[21] He appears to have decided with his inner circle that his term of office should now be extended from ten years to life, but that the impetus must appear to come from below. It was launched from the Tribunate, remodelled in the course of the spring to ease the passage of the concordat and the peace treaties. On 6 May 1802 the newly pliant tribunes voted that the first consul should be offered 'a shining token of national gratitude' for all his achievements. They urged the Legislative Body and the Senate to support them and sent a deputation to convey their resolution to the Tuileries. The first consul received them with republican modesty: 'I desire no other glory than that of having entirely fulfilled the task imposed on me. I aspire to no other reward than the affection of my fellow citizens.'[22] He said the same to members of the Senate. He thought they understood him well enough to offer him consulship for life. He was wrong. Most senators believed that he would be satisfied with a guaranteed second ten-year term, and this was almost universally agreed. Napoleon was stunned. He had thought that 'the majority of the Senate is always ready to do more than they are asked.'[23] It took all the persuasive ability of the wily Cambacérès to calm him down into accepting a fallback strategy. While the first consul pointedly absented himself at Malmaison, his colleague convoked the Council of State to discuss the extension of the consular term. Any change, Cambacérès argued, should be endorsed like the original consular constitution by national consent in a plebiscite. The question, however, should not be about a ten-year extension, but the consulship for life. This raised in acute form the further question of the succession. As Roederer (a key figure in the discussion) had long been suggesting, it was proposed that the first consul should be authorized to name his own successor.

Yet Napoleon still baulked at this. Aware, no doubt, of the well-established doctrine that only despots tried to name their own successors, he also knew of the unpropitious historical precedents. Dead men had no authority, he said; even the will of Louis XIV had been overturned. In any case, he still could not think of anybody who deserved to succeed him. So that when the draft plan was presented to him, he struck out the succession question. Meanwhile, to avoid the earlier unpredictable clumsiness of the Senate, the plebiscite was authorized by consular decree alone. The nation was simply asked whether Napoleon Bonaparte should be made first consul for life. Local officials were instructed to ensure a large turnout, and it was certainly more impressive, or at least more discreetly handled, than the vote in favour of the consular constitution in 1799. The result, proclaimed in the Senate on 4 August 1802, was 3,568,885 in favour, to 8,374 against. Even discounting some precautionary gerrymandering, this was a solid endorsement, reflecting a participation rate of around 40 per cent of the electorate. Napoleon was well satisfied. 'From this moment', he told Thibaudeau (who had voted against), 'I am on the same level as other sovereigns; because in the end they too are only there for their lifetime.'[24] And Fouché, who understood public opinion better than anyone, recalled in his memoirs that 'Most of the citizens who had voted to confer the supreme magistracy on him for life believed that they were bringing the monarchical system back to France, and with him rest and stability.'[25]

Rest and stability would prove fleeting, but monarchy was certainly back. It was decided to reinforce the life consulate with further constitutional changes. The very day after the results of the plebiscite were announced, a senatorial act (senatusconsultum) of 86 clauses, almost as long as the original constitution itself, finally endowed the first consul for life with the right to name his successor, either during his lifetime or by a document to be opened at his death. The two other consuls were also made life appointments, but on the nomination of the first. Under what was soon known as the Constitution of the Year x, the head of state's powers over every level of government were vastly widened. He was granted the classic kingly prerogative of clemency and endowed with a new level of policy making in the form of a Privy Council, an old regime name for a tight handful of handpicked advisers. The powers and procedures of the two legislative chambers, already trimmed and purged during the spring, were further curtailed. Only the Senate, the official source of this new 'constitution', retained its central role in government – although even here the first consul increased his say in its composition and recruitment.

Meanwhile, all the foreign tourists who poured into France that summer remarked on the growing splendour of the consular court. Records were combed, and the memories of ageing servants of the old monarchy racked, to find precedents for how a court should be organized, right down to how courtiers should dress. It was soon noted by knowledgeable observers that the new court was far more ceremonious and rigidly organized than the old, and certainly outshone those of contemporary monarchs. A sharp-eyed Mme de Staël observed that, as early as October 1801, when the appointment of his brother-in-law to command the Saint-Domingue expedition was announced, Napoleon used the royal plural.[26]

A further monarchical indicator was an enhanced role for the first consul's wife. Joséphine had always been opposed to the life consulship. She was afraid that sooner or later it would pose the question of heredity, aware as she was that she was now too old to have more children, and that most of her husband's blood relatives hated her. There were constant rumours and suggestions of a divorce. But, for the moment, Napoleon valued her support. He readily agreed early in 1802 to the marriage of her daughter, Hortense, to his brother Louis. It was a stormy, loveless match, but to his obvious delight, they produced a Bonaparte son, whom he saw as a potential heir. Meanwhile, Joséphine was assigned ladies-in-waiting, and, in processions, walked ahead of the other two consuls. At public receptions she welcomed the waves of guests as a prelude to the culminating appearance of her husband. And increasingly these formal occasions took place not only at the Tuileries but in the refurbished Palace of Saint-Cloud, high above Paris to the west, where the young general had first seized power just three years earlier.

* * *

IN ALL BUT name, France had a king again. The problem of executive authority, which began in 1789 with the assertion of a national sovereignty, had at last been settled – although not in the way that the men of 1789 had intended. Instead of a constitutional monarchy, Napoleon had recreated an absolute one. It was true that his regime embodied written constitutions, but unlike their revolutionary predecessors they served to enhance rather than circumscribe executive authority. The three legislative chambers were unelected, existing to endorse rather than formulate legislation, and easily silenced or overridden at the first sign of dissent or resistance.

Whether Napoleon would have remained content (like a Fifth Republic president) to exercise monarchical power without a crown seems unlikely but uncertain. At least there were no further steps towards ultimate enthronement so long as the peace of 1802 lasted. But when the peace broke down, after barely a year, the fragility of a regime as dependent as ever on one man's life became, once more, an urgent issue. In Brittany, chouans began to stir again, and their most intransigent leader, Georges Cadoudal, returned from England with promises of financial backing for new assassination attempts. Early in 1804 a grand plan was uncovered to kidnap the first consul and import an unnamed Bourbon prince. Orchestrated by Cadoudal, it had attempted to recruit Moreau, the victor of Hohenlinden known for his hostility to Napoleon, to the 'General Monck' role that the latter had spurned in 1800. Focus though he was, and knew himself to be, of the hopes of all who opposed Napoleon, Moreau soon disappointed the plotters. If they succeeded, he obviously hoped to take power for himself, and not the Bourbons, but he refused to involve himself actively in their plans. Meanwhile, the details of the conspiracy were soon known to the police, and its main agents, including a resurgent Pichegru and eventually Cadoudal himself, were arrested. The opportunity was taken to arrest Moreau, too. Pichegru met a mysterious death in prison. Cadoudal proudly confessed his guilt, and went to the guillotine shouting 'Vive le Roi!' Napoleon clearly wanted the same fate for Moreau; but even handpicked judges could find no convincing evidence of capital crime. Eventually they sentenced him to two years in prison. That was all you got, Napoleon raged, for stealing handkerchiefs! But it was clear that there was widespread sympathy for Moreau, especially in the army. Reluctantly, his jealous rival commuted his sentence to exile, and Moreau spent the next nine years in America. Even so, he did eventually die at Napoleon's hands, killed by a French cannonball as he fought against the emperor at the Battle of Leipzig in 1813.

Meanwhile, the life consul had sent his ultimate riposte to the Bourbons. Interrogation of the arrested conspirators had revealed that their plot was intended to culminate in the arrival of an unnamed royal prince. The most likely candidate seemed to be the Duc d'Enghien, grandson of the oldest and most inveterate of the émigrés, the Prince de Condé. He was living just across the Rhine from Strasbourg. The evidence was thin; the supposition strong. It was enough to impel the first consul to order a snatch squad to kidnap the duke and bring him on to French territory. Once there, he was rushed to Paris and immediately brought before a military court, accused of being in British pay and bearing arms against France. It was made clear to the judges that a capital sentence was expected. No sooner was it delivered than it was carried out. In the small hours of 20 March 1804, Enghien was shot and buried in the ditch of the Château of Vincennes. Years later, Napoleon recalled ordering the execution: 'When they tried to murder me, I simply had to take reprisals.'[27] There was now a blood feud between the House of Bourbon and what was about to become the House of Bonaparte.

Monarchical Europe was horrified but also cowed by French power. Although no state allowed the publication of Louis XVIII's anguished protest, which he had tried to issue from a ship in the international waters of the Baltic, the cynical murder of Enghien sowed the seeds of a new anti-French coalition, which would take shape in 1805. In France, however, the deed attracted far less public interest than the fate of Cadoudal and Moreau as they awaited trial; and above all, the final transformation of the life consul into a full-blown monarch. The return of plots against his life had finally prompted Napoleon to grasp a crown. He revealed his decision to intimates only days after the execution of Enghien. At once the entire machinery of government set about engineering statements of support. 'Great man,' the Senate urged him, 'finish your work by making it as immortal as your glory . . . You have rescued us from past chaos, you have vouchsafed us our present benefits, give us a guarantee for the future.'[28] The legislative chambers echoed the call, as did concerted addresses from the departments and (particularly reassuringly) from the army. All were published in the government-controlled press. By early April the Privy Council was discussing what to call the new monarch. Bestriding the continent, his realm buttressed by obedient satellites, he was surely more than a king, more like a new Charlemagne, nothing less than an emperor. When the news reached his prison cell, Cadoudal observed sardonically: 'I have done better than I hoped. I wanted to give France a king, and I have given her an Emperor.'[29] The change was formally proclaimed in a senatusconsultum of 18 May 1804 – still officially 28 Floréal, Year XII.

This reflected an ambiguity in the very first clause of the senatusconsultum, soon to be called the Constitution of the Year XII. The state which the emperor and his natural or adoptive heirs male was to rule was still called a republic. The name was retained in the oath taken by the emperor at his coronation, in those taken by all imperial officials and in the formula for the promulgation of laws. But the new dynasty was also declared to rule by the grace of God, like any true royalty. Dating by the republican calendar only lasted two more years, and the year after that, all references to the Republic in official documents were quietly dropped. Yet in the coronation oath, taken by the emperor at a lavish ceremony in Notre Dame on 2 December 1804, certain revolutionary commitments still survived. The imperial monarch pledged to respect religious, political and civil liberty, to raise taxation only by law and maintain the irrevocability of the sale of national lands. And, as in 1799, although the new constitution came into force immediately, it was submitted to a confirmatory plebiscite. The results were somewhat disappointing. Although 4,000 more voters said yes than in 1802, and votes against fell by almost 6,000 to a paltry 2,596, without the well-managed votes of new territories acquired at the Peace of Amiens, and those of the army, the outcome would have demonstrated less enthusiasm for an emperor than for a life consul. But the nation, declared sovereign in 1789, had been openly consulted, and agreed by a convincing (if managed) margin to be ruled once again by a hereditary monarch. 'You French,' the Corsican adventurer told his intimates, now his subjects, as they contemplated his new status, 'you love monarchy, it's the only government that you like.'[30] Despite lingering verbal ambiguities, France's republican experiment was over for another half century; and the last of the three great wounds inflicted on the nation by its revolution was, for the moment, closed up.

5

Curbing Disorder

Born and raised on an island notorious for its brigands, Napoleon knew what lawlessness meant. Yet he hated disorder. He was appalled as he witnessed the Parisian tumults, which had marked the last weeks of the monarchy, and was always prepared to admit privately that popular uprisings scared him. In 1795 he was actually briefly cashiered from the army for refusing a posting on internal police duties in the rebellious Vendée, and only rescued from this disgrace when Barras recruited him to command troops against the Vendémiaire royalist insurrection in Paris. But this at least, he recalled, was a *political* insurrection that one could 'mow down without pity . . . with twelve hundred well-led men and four cannon'.[1] It was, however, extremely difficult in revolutionary France to decide which disorders were political and which not. The problem was exemplified on the very eve of Napoleonic rule, as the conqueror of Egypt began his triumphal journey from the coast of Provence to Paris in the second week of October 1799. In the old provincial capital of Aix, he was welcomed by enthusiastic crowds; but when his baggage train followed shortly afterwards, the wagons were pillaged and stripped by brigands.

Revolutions break the law by definition. They would not be needed if change could be achieved legally. And in one sense the Revolution of 1789 in France was a nationwide outburst of lawlessness which the normal forces of order proved helpless to contain. Politically under attack, traditional social and judicial authority seemed paralysed; and even the ultimate instrument of power, the army, was unreliable. Mutinous troops played a vital role in the storming of the Bastille, and the king was advised that the rest might not obey orders. That may have been a fatal misjudgement, but over the next three years, military discipline certainly crumbled in many regiments. After sovereignty passed from the king to the nation, the chain of command was no longer clear. Oath-bound to the monarch, many noble officers hesitated in their allegiance to new authority, while the increasingly anti-aristocratic rhetoric of the Revolution eroded the obedience of the ranks to their superiors. Soldiers flocked to join Jacobin clubs, where they were often encouraged to question their orders. Military support was increasingly called in to preserve or restore public calm, but it could no longer be relied on. Even the young Napoleon spent more time intriguing in Corsica than with his mainland units, and eventually it was assumed that, like so many of his brother officers, he had given up and emigrated. Reintegrated on reappearing in Paris, within weeks he disappeared again to Corsica, only returning to France in June 1793 with his family when their lives came under threat. It took until then for him to commit himself completely to the service of the Republic.

Military disarray was most vividly displayed in August 1790, when some of the garrison of Nancy mutinied. The outbreak was put down by other troops with exemplary severity, but the affair polarized opinion. A number of the mutineers were executed, and others sent to the galleys. A year later, however, the general who suppressed the outbreak, the Marquis de Bouillé, emigrated, having tried in vain to help the king escape in the Flight to Varennes. And a year later still, the imprisoned mutineers were pardoned by the Legislative Assembly and welcomed to Paris by cheering crowds. It was true that, after a disastrous start, the army began to redeem itself against foreign enemies later in 1792, but fighting them absorbed most of its time and manpower over the next two years. The absence of reliable armed protection does much to explain the weakness of the Convention when confronted by the armed and organized sansculottes.

In 1789 suspicion of the army, combined with fear of anarchy, prompted the spontaneous formation of citizen militias, which coalesced over the subsequent winter into the National Guard. Initially made up largely of rich volunteers with property to defend, the showy expensive uniforms and parades of the Guard did little to guarantee stable public order. When the women of Paris forced the royal family to relocate from Versailles to the capital in October 1789, all the National Guard could do was lamely escort the triumphant insurgents and their hostages back to the city. From the start, there was rivalry between guards and regular soldiers, and their voluntary status made them just as likely to disobey orders as ordinary troops now were. In April 1791 National Guards defied their commander, Lafayette, to side with suspicious crowds to prevent the royal family leaving Paris for Easter. 'Individuals have been seen preaching anarchy' reported the departmental administrators of the Tarn department early in 1792,

> In seeking to assert that all official authorities should give way to the wishes of a few assembled citizens: by these false ideas agitators are misleading the populace: national guards, forgetting their first duty, far from deploying the force vested in them for the maintenance of calm, have made appalling use of it to uphold and favour citizens in rebellion for whom persons and properties are no longer at all sacred.[2]

The best-known action of the Parisian Guards on the side of public order, the massacre of republican petitioners on 17 July 1791, was a public relations disaster, whose memory was only expunged by the opening of their ranks a year later to all citizens regardless of wealth or property. And by the time of the Convention, the capital's National Guard, so far from protecting the nation's representatives from intimidation by the sansculottes, was little more than the best-armed instrument of popular power.

The initial successes of the Revolution had lent instinctive legitimacy to defiance of authority at every level. Popular disorder in the countryside and attacks on lordly property, exacerbated by the 'Great Fear' of July 1789, were the spur to the comprehensive surrender of privileges on the night of 4 August – the most radical legislative session of the entire Revolution. The example encouraged the belief that anything might be achieved by the threat or use of violence. Belligerent language suffused public discourse, and self-styled patriots in their Jacobin clubs felt entitled to promote the nation's cause by threatening its enemies. In this atmosphere, and in the absence of effective policing, criminality of all sorts flourished, to the despair of older authorities, and indeed many of the new. If unprecedented disorder marked the early months of the Revolution, however, it only reinforced a deeper commitment among its founding fathers to the idea of the rule of law. Law, proclaimed the Declaration of the Rights of Man and the Citizen, is the expression of the nation's general will, and the primacy of law was invoked in no fewer than nine of its seventeen clauses. There was constant talk throughout the work of the Constituent Assembly of comprehensive legal reform – although this aspiration was only brought to fruition under the rule of Napoleon.

Meanwhile, all the well-meaning reforms of the preceding months, complained the procurator-general of the Parlement of Bordeaux in February 1790, 'have only produced until now evils difficult to count. Liberty, that sentiment so natural to mankind, has for some been a mere principle of seduction. Murderous hordes are ravaging parts of our region. Such are the first fruits of a liberty proclaimed before the law that should set its limits.'[3] Outraged local patriots, however, denounced the hapless magistrate to the National

Assembly which, in predictably censuring him, disclaimed responsibility for any disorder. It was easier to blame the machinations of counter-revolutionaries. Either way, however, the disorder was real enough. More than 4,000 popular disturbances shook the French countryside between 1789 and 1792 – half as many as had occurred in towns and country combined over the preceding 140 years. And the early years of the Revolution saw a massive rise in petty crime in the cities. Thefts in Paris more than doubled, crimes of violence quadrupled. One reason was obviously disarray among the forces of law and order, as a dizzying stream of reforms disrupted every layer of authority and enforcement. Another was a sudden rise in unemployment resulting from the shrinkage of noble households and the buying habits of their embattled (or emigrated) owners, not to mention the confiscation of Church properties and the closure of ecclesiastical corporations such as chapters and monasteries. Poverty and crime were always closely linked. The population of France rose by almost 2 million over the revolutionary decade, in a context of constant economic crisis and soaring inflation as massive overissue of paper money in the form of assignats debauched the currency. At the same time, successive revolutionary assemblies steadily removed the main source of poor relief through their dismantling of the institutional wealth of the Church. And the impact on public order of the revolutionary quarrel with the Church was not simply economic. When the oath of 1790 tore the clergy apart it polarized the laity too. Refusers of the oath, and the faithful laity who supported them, were increasingly branded as public enemies defying the law. The accelerating stream of punitive sanctions against refractory priests identified them as one of the main vectors of disorder. Seducing their former parishioners from the constitutional church, inciting them to persecute oath-takers, not to mention buyers of former church lands, the nonjurors invoked the authority of the pope and God Himself to justify lawlessness. Legislators, patriotic local authorities and Jacobin clubs in their turn denounced them as 'fanatics', and their followers not just as criminals and rebels but as suspects and traitors – especially after the outbreak of war. And when the monarchy, and with it the Constitution of 1791, was overthrown on 10 August 1792 by popular violence, it set the same example as in 1789. Self-appointed patriots all over the country took the law into their own hands to intimidate and thwart the perceived agents of counter-revolution, royalism and the nonjuring priests who gave them inspiration. The notorious climax came with the Paris prison massacres of early September, when nonjuror priests were the preferred victims. After this, for much of the first year of its existence, the Convention sat in fear of massacre at the hands of Paris militants. How to avoid it was the underlying source of division between Girondins and Montagnards: the former thought the sansculottes should be resisted, the latter that they must be appeased. Fear of what they might do did much to determine the fate of the dethroned king, for whom the sansculottes demanded nothing less than death. And it was popular pressure, in alliance with a democratized National Guard, which forced the Convention to purge itself of the sansculottes' leading Girondin critics in June 1793.

The background to this was incipient civil war. In western districts, attempts to evict nonjuring priests from their livings had provoked widespread rioting ever since 1791. This and popular resentments of other changes imposed by the Revolution was compounded in the spring of 1793 by the introduction of selective military service. An expanding number of foreign enemies and a decline in patriotic volunteering led the Convention to decree the call-up of 300,000 able-bodied young men to the armies – a measure which fell heaviest on the mainstay of the rural workforce, provoking defiance and outrage throughout the country, and in Brittany and the Vendée it was met with armed resistance. Breton peasant attacks on the urban hubs of republican authority were quickly repulsed, but gave way to far less controllable banditry in the countryside, known as *chouannerie*. In the Vendée, south of the Loire, rebels soon coalesced into a full-blown 'Catholic and Royal Army', offering defiance to the whole Revolution. And meanwhile, as the military triumphs of the previous autumn were reversed and Belgium and the Rhineland evacuated, major provincial cities became restive at the domination of the nation's representatives by the bloodthirsty perpetrators of the September massacres. The expulsion of the Girondins from the Convention pushed them into open resistance. Over the summer, Lyon, Marseille, Bordeaux, Caen and Toulon mounted what the Montagnards called a 'federalist' revolt against the power of Paris. Toulon, the great Mediterranean naval port, even surrendered to the British. News of this ultimate treason, arriving early in September, once more brought the sansculottes out to mob the Convention. They demanded that government by terror should now be the order of the day.

The Convention responded by licensing patriotic violence. Watch committees, set up earlier, were now empowered to arrest and imprison anybody they considered suspicious. In southern areas, where vendetta was an established reflex of local rivalries, this only reinforced old tendencies with new layers of resentment. Meanwhile, so-called 'revolutionary armies' of urban militants were dispatched into the countryside to terrorize peasants into releasing food supplies to the towns. There was no check on their depredations. As one deputy told local patriots in Poitiers, 'You can do anything, get anything, break anything, smash anything, shoot anything, judge anything, dump anything, guillotine anything . . . Don't fucking wait.'[4] It is true that the Convention sent out its own members on missions to reinforce or restore its authority across the country, but they had to begin by endorsing much direct action that merely looked patriotic. 'We ought to behave like brigands,' declared one determined deputy, and not all his hearers were shocked. Some representatives on mission positively encouraged attacks on churches and all signs of religious commitment, which they saw as the heart of counter-revolution. The violent, often chaotic dechristianization of that autumn originated in the persecution of priests and closure of churches sponsored by representatives like Fouché.

But before the end of the year, this anarchic phase of terror was coming to an end as the centres of so-called federalism surrendered and punishment of leading rebels began. As the 'revolutionary government', proclaimed and invested with plenary powers in October, gradually achieved a monopoly of legitimate violence, terror became bureaucratized, and repression was administered by special tribunals. Although they often returned not guilty verdicts, these courts also sent over 16,000 victims to spectacular death by the guillotine. The prospect of a resolute and self-confident authority, unafraid to restore order by shedding blood, and now buttressed by increasing numbers of regular troops raised under the *levée en masse* decreed in August 1793, was enough to slow the spread of random opportunistic violence. In the Vendée, after the defeat of the last Catholic and Royal Army at Savenay in December 1793, its home territory was systematically ravaged over the next spring by 'infernal columns' of soldiery empowered to visit indiscriminate terror on the entire population, reducing survivors to sullen hatred of the Republic. These savageries only lasted a few months, but no amount of conciliatory changes could expunge their bitter memory. It kept sporadic anti-revolutionary violence simmering throughout the western departments for another decade.

In Paris, meanwhile, the apparently triumphant sansculottes were slowly tamed by their integration into government service. Attempts to mobilize them against the Convention in March 1794 were easily squashed, and that same month the marauding *armées révolutionnaires* were disbanded. And allies of Robespierre, outlawed by his fellow deputies and barricaded in the Hôtel de Ville on 9 Thermidor, appealed for sansculotte support to save him, the small number who responded soon melted away in the face of forces loyal to the Convention.

Terror, pressed on the Convention by the threat of popular violence, had considerably curbed that violence even as it saved the Revolution from overthrow. But it had to be stopped. Nobody thought that terror could possibly be a permanent way of running the country. Nobody had given more thought to ways of bringing it to an end than Robespierre, as Napoleon later recognized. He was brought down, the emperor asserted, not because he was a tyrant, but because he wanted to conclude the Revolution and 'put an end to so much blood'.[5] However that might be, he was a convenient scapegoat; and upon his downfall the machinery of terror was steadily dismantled. Within months, thousands of resentful suspects had been released from imprisonment: the watch committees that had put them there were systematically downgraded, and special tribunals dissolved. The paradoxical result, however, was that, so far from ending the bloodshed, this retreat from state violence merely removed the restraints that terror had imposed on general disorder and crime. In Paris, bands of well-dressed conservative thugs, the so-called 'gilded youth' (*jeunesse dorée*), emerged to harass and beat up former sansculotte militants, unrestrained by any action from the Convention. And when, amid the soaring inflation and famine conditions of the freezing spring of 1795, the remnants of sansculotte militancy attempted, in the insurrections of Germinal, and Prairial, to coerce the legislators as of old into restoring the controlled economy of the Year II, empty promises, in response, were followed by a decree disarming former Jacobin officials and placing them under house arrest, where they could easily be targeted. Compliant newspapers listed their names. It proved the trigger for a massive wave of revenge killings throughout the south, the so-called White Terror, in which around 2,000 victims identified as former terrorists, or 'blood drinkers', perished. Attacks ranged from isolated incidents to prison massacres every bit as bloody as those in Paris in September 1792. Returned émigrés, profiting from a partial amnesty, played a part in some incidents, but private vengeance was a more powerful driver than counter-revolution. Resistance to military service, which had triggered the initial uprising in the Vendée, was now a pervasive problem almost everywhere. Young men who had dodged the draft, or deserted the colours, turned readily to crime to support themselves, often organized into notorious gangs of cut-throats (*égorgeurs*) or *chauffeurs*, who tortured their victims by holding their feet to fires. Highway robbery was a constant complaint of all travellers. And although the west was somewhat pacified over the spring by a series of treaties with leaders of the Vendéans or chouans, endemic disorder continued. Young General Bonaparte's reluctance to be redeployed to the Vendée was perhaps compounded when his horse, sent there in preparation, was stolen by chouans. 'It is to be hoped', he wrote to his brother Joseph, 'that soon a firm and better organized government will put a stop to all this.'[6]

That was certainly his hope for the directorial regime, which he helped to establish two months later when he crushed the insurrection of Vendémiaire. Dispatched soon afterwards to his destiny in Italy, he was not in France to see that hope disappointed. The Constitution of the Year III was designed to establish an uncontested republican government. Endorsed by a referendum, it sought to expunge the Revolution's bitter legacies. Yet it was created by the same Convention that had authorized government by terror, and the deputies had so little faith in its durability that they perpetuated their own rule through the Two-Thirds Law. The very last act of the Convention was to proclaim an amnesty for anyone convicted of 'offences concerning the Revolution' – but it, and other legislation passed the day before, explicitly excluded émigrés and their relatives, the rebels of Vendémiaire and nonjuring priests. Consequently, royalists and counter-revolutionaries were offered no encouragement to support the new constitution. And although, to counteract this, Jacobins imprisoned and persecuted after the demonstrations of Germinal and Prairial were released and allowed back into public life, many of them, too, found the new order unacceptable. Within six months, Gracchus Babeuf and his Jacobin co-conspirators were alarming the new regime amid rumours of a plot to overthrow it. General Bonaparte's last public appearance, only days before his marriage and departure for Italy, was in command of troops closing down the Pantheon Club, where Babeuf and his allies hoped to rally support in the spirit of the long-defunct Jacobins. The Directory's thwarting of their 'Conspiracy of Equals' some weeks later, at the very moment of his first Italian victories, brought a new indulgence towards those excluded from the earlier amnesties, and this coincided with an expectation among them that the first elections scheduled for the spring of 1797 would bring an opportunity to turn back the work of the Revolution by non-violent means. Many royalists turned from organizing crime to organizing votes. In the west, after the bloody defeat of the Quiberon invasion of the summer of 1795, General Lazare Hoche brought an atmosphere of relative calm by allowing the reopening of churches, sometimes even served by refractory priests, alongside ruthless pursuit of persistent chouans by 'flying columns', culminating in the spring of 1796 in the capture and execution of their best-known leaders, Jean-Nicolas Stofflet and François Charette. But everyday disorder continued. 'Many deserters are lurking in the woods,' reported an English diplomatic visitor passing through Chantilly in November 1796, 'and there are continual robberies and murders. We have not travelled half an hour in the dark.'[7] Very wisely, for much of the country seemed to be infested by violent brigands with no particular political aims. The roads of the northeast and Normandy were notorious for the depredations of organized bands of highwaymen. The fearsome bande d'Orgères of over one hundred members, terrorizing country to the southwest of the capital, was responsible for 75 murders between 1791 and 1798. And Paris itself, that same diplomat noted on arrival, was 'without police [and] full of robbers and murderers'.[8]

By the next summer, the city was also full of royalist guerrilla captains, brought together by a secret emissary from Louis XVIII. The spring elections, as expected, had produced a conservative landslide, but as the new deputies began to make their reactionary intentions clear, victorious generals like Hoche and Bonaparte began to fear that their triumphs might be squandered in a peace with Bourbon-supporting powers. They made their concerns obvious, and it was this that brought so many chouan and Vendéan leaders to Paris in order to counteract a possible military coup. But the generals and sympathetic directors struck first in the purge of Fructidor, before the new legislators had steeled themselves to accepting the protection of armed irregulars. The plotters scattered back to their western power bases.

Constitutional royalism had obviously failed. Armed resistance was once again the only option for counter-revolutionaries, and they were positively driven to it by the 'Directorial Terror' that followed Fructidor, with its renewed persecution of nonjuring priests and returned émigrés. The 'Second Directory' also struck at non-political brigandage. In January 1798 the law of 29 Nivôse, Year VI set up a structure of military courts with extensive civil powers, more expeditious than ordinary criminal courts, and less inclined, with no juries, to leniency. It also extended the range of capital offences. The relative international peace of 1797–8 released regular troops for internal police duties to back up the new courts, but this reinforcement did not last. In the spring of 1798 General Bonaparte took the flower of the Republic's armies off on his Egyptian adventure. This in turn began to bring France's enemies together again and made it urgent to rebuild armies whose strength had halved since the days of the *levée en masse* in 1793–4. After months of debate, in September 1798 the councils passed the Jourdan Law on conscription, and within three weeks the 'class of 1778' was summoned to the colours. Six months later, with French forces in full retreat across Italy, Switzerland and Germany, two more classes were hastily called up. This law would form the basis of French military recruitment for much of the next century. Napoleon regarded it as the bedrock of his military machine, and conscription as quite the best way to build up a spirited fighting force. 'It made the French army', he reminisced on St Helena, 'the best formed ever. It was ... an eminently national institution ... only mothers are still upset by it.'⁹

But this was never true, and never less so than when conscription was introduced. There was massive resistance. The legislators themselves were well aware of how unpopular it would be. Remembering how the 1793 calls to arms had triggered western rebellion, they actually exempted nine notorious departments from the new law. But some areas, such as the departments of the recently annexed Belgium, had never before known any form of compulsory recruitment. Already alienated (like the Vendée in 1793) by persecution of nonjuring priests and the confiscation of the Church's wealth, the new departments of Flanders broke into outright rebellion in October 1798. At one point the number of insurgents reached 10,000, coalescing briefly into a peasant army. Its heyday was brief. By December it had been defeated, with savage reprisals. But conscription continued to be widely defied through draft-dodging (*insoumission*) or desertion on the road to enrolment. By the time Napoleon took power, 5,000 Belgians had been successfully drafted, but the initial target had been 22,000. The story was similar across the Republic. One of the more popular gains of the early Revolution among the peasantry had been the abolition in 1791 of service in the militia, recruited by drawing lots. The Jourdan Law marked the return of this procedure, leading to service far more demanding than the part-time reserve functions of the old militia. In eastern areas that were long accustomed to providing military volunteers, districts had few problems providing their quotas; but in remoter regions far from the frontiers, ballot-evasion was a serious problem, not to mention desertion among recruits on the road to their assigned units. And whereas draft evaders could often slip back into their receptive villages after the draw, the obvious temptation for deserters far from home was brigandage, especially when they could take their government-provided weapons with them.

By the spring of 1799, therefore, the Republic appeared to be in a crisis as severe as that of 1793. Its best general was marooned with a shrinking army in Egypt, its domination of Italy crumbling in the face of generalized revolt, a new coalition of foreign powers poised to invade its territory and internal disorder everywhere as the state struggled to mobilize its human resources for all-out war. And despite directorial efforts to manipulate the annual legislative elections in by-now routine fashion, this time they brought an influx of left-leaning deputies attracted by the sort of draconian reflexes that had saved the Republic in the Year II. Equating all forms of brigandage with counter-revolution, in July the new councils passed a 'law on the repression of brigandage and murder in the interior' which stipulated that in areas 'notoriously in a troubled civil state' the local authorities might take hostage relatives of émigrés, nobles and anyone else known for opposing the Revolution, as security for the good behaviour of their districts. Echoes of the Law of Suspects of 1793 were unmistakeable. For every murder committed, five hostages might be deported, their property confiscated and a heavy fine shared between all hostages. In practice, this law was sparingly applied, but its symbolic impact was enormous. It alarmed everyone who dreaded a return to terror; and so far from deterring disorder, as one chouan captain recalled, it 'did more for the party in two weeks than all the initiatives we undertook in several months of touring the region'.[10]

The 'party' in question was a counter-revolutionary plan for co-ordinated action between the coalition powers; royalist plotters organized under a so-called 'Swabian agency' and operating through the revived remnants of the 'philanthropic institutes' of 1797; and the chouan bands of the west. It was impossibly ambitious but alarming enough viewed from Paris. Although planned to come into simultaneous effect in August 1799 as the coalition's armies, building on their seemingly easy victories of the spring, were expected to sweep into France, the plot sputtered prematurely into life as philanthropic institutes across the south proved unable to control the anti-republican zeal of their expectant members. Over the spring, there were increasing reports of murders of republicans, attacks on convoys carrying state funds and destruction of symbolic liberty trees. Full-blown insurrection finally burst out around Toulouse in the first days of August. Ten thousand militarily organized insurgents tried to storm the city, but after a four-day siege the attack was repulsed. For the next few weeks much of the southwest was engulfed in guerrilla warfare. By the end of the month, however, republican forces had the upper hand, and the last organized royalist force had been destroyed. Over 4,000 rebels had been killed and 6,000 captured and interned. Special courts were established to bring them rapidly to trial, but the prisons of Toulouse were still full of untried royalist captives at the time of the Brumaire coup.

It was true that throughout July and August French forces continued to suffer the expected defeats at the hands of the coalition, but so too did their enemies fail to move on towards an invasion, so the planned convergence of foreign and domestic counter-revolution never materialized. Yet in order to protect the frontiers, large numbers of troops were transferred from internal policing, which made attempts at repression relatively ineffective. Alarmed by the defeat of royalism in the southwest, the leaders of Breton and Norman chouans met on 15 September and, before it was too late, proclaimed a royalist uprising of what they called the 'Malcontents'. Encouraged and subsidized from England, they were far more effectively organized than previous chouans. Within a month, on the very day that Napoleon arrived back in Paris (14 October), 3,000 of them stormed and pillaged Le Mans. It was the greatest success in the entire history of *chouannerie*. Yet the rebels only controlled the city for four days, and although over the next fortnight a number of other important towns were attacked, none of them was taken. The tide now turned decisively against the royalist grand design. The Austro-Russian offensive had been stopped at Zurich late in September, and an Anglo-Russian invasion of the Batavian Republic had been repulsed. Both French victories released seasoned troops for deployment to the disturbed districts of the west. Their task was made easier by the news of Napoleon's seizure of power. Like almost everybody at first, counter-revolutionaries were unsure what to make of it. Many hoped that it presaged a restoration of monarchy, which would make further efforts on their part unnecessary. And the general now in overall command of the Republic's forces in the western departments, Gabriel Joseph d'Hédouville, experienced from earlier service under Hoche in dealing with chouans, decided to pursue conciliation rather than increased repression. Everyone was waiting to see what France's new ruler might do.

* * *

AMID ALL THE pressing business of organizing a new government, the general found time for a spectacular show of magnanimity. Three days after taking power, he rescinded the Law of Hostages. To emphasize the importance of the deed, he went in person to the Temple – the main state prison since the destruction of the Bastille – and set free a group of hostages held there. 'An unjust law', he grandiloquently declared, 'has deprived you of freedom; my first gesture is to restore it to you.'[11] Everyone, except perhaps militant Jacobins, could welcome this. It said little, however, about how the new regime might confront the problem of disorder in the country at large. Napoleon's instincts were authoritarian, but he was already proud of coming to power without bloodshed, and he chose at first to find out for himself what the western rebels might accept for ending their defiance. As Hédouville laboriously negotiated an armistice and called off repressive operations, chouan leaders invited to Paris for a secret meeting with the first consul were told he had no intention of restoring the Bourbons. But he offered to restore and guarantee full freedom of worship and to pardon all rebels who laid down their arms. 'Too much French blood', he declared in a follow-up letter, 'has already flowed over ten years', and no enlightened man of honour could fail to support a government determined to restore order, justice and true liberty.

> So say clearly to your fellow citizens that revolutionary laws
> will no longer come to devastate the fair land of France,
> that the Revolution is over, that freedom of conscience
> will be entire and absolute, that protection will be equal
> for all citizens and independent of any sort of prejudice.[12]

But he made no mention of royalist aspirations; and in a general proclamation to the western departments issued the day before, he denounced the two brothers of Louis xvi as cowardly traitors in English pay. To true patriotic citizens, however, he offered the end of unjust laws and arbitrary rule, redress for those wrongly listed as émigrés, revocation of forced loans and the Law of Hostages and protection for agriculture.

Nevertheless, he concluded with a threat. If, despite all these promises, some were still determined to foment civil war, then the government would resort to the 'sad necessity' of force. In fact, Napoleon had never truly believed in the good faith of the chouans negotiating with Hédouville. The commitment to a royalist restoration of those he met in person had been clear and unshakeable. So, even as he urged the west to make peace, he ordered preparations to be made for renewed repression. 'The confidence of the Government in general Hédouville is entire,' he told the war minister, 'but he must not allow himself to be distracted any longer.'[13] If no further progress was made, with 40,000 men at his disposal, he was to suspend the constitution in disturbed departments and do whatever it took to restore order. The truce that Hédouville had negotiated was due to expire on 23 January 1800 (1 Pluviôse), and in any case Georges Cadoudal, the fiercest of the chouan commanders, had never signed it. A week before the expiry, General Guillaume Brune, fresh from victories over the British in Holland, was placed in command over Hédouville, with orders to suspend constitutional guarantees in four disturbed departments and make Cadoudal's territory in the Morbihan in particular 'feel the whole weight and horrors of war', by burning farms and villages and living off the land.[14] 'It is only by making war terrible for them that the inhabitants will themselves turn against the brigands.' And the moment the truce expired, a simultaneous blitz of mobile terror squads was launched across the whole heartland of *chouannerie*. 'The goal of your conduct should be this,' the first consul instructed Hédouville, 'to act so that in the months of Ventôse and Germinal, when the sea becomes less stormy, when part of our troops will be called towards the Rhine, there shall be nobody left in the departments of the West with the power and the strength to revolt and back . . . enemies.'[15] No seaborne invasion from England like that of Quiberon in 1795 could then hope to threaten the eastern offensives planned for the coming summer.

The strategy worked. Within weeks, most of the chouan bands had laid down their arms. By mid-February even Cadoudal had come to terms, and the last remaining Norman leader, Louis de Frotté, was negotiating his own capitulation. But when he refused to disarm, Napoleon decided that a spectacular example must be made. Despite negotiating under safe conduct, Frotté, with six of his comrades, was brought before a military tribunal, which knew what the first consul wanted. He was condemned to be shot. By this time, hundreds of other chouans had lost their lives; but the great onslaught had succeeded. To celebrate the achievement, but also to separate them from their followers, the remaining chouan leaders were once more invited to Paris. The first consul made a special point of meeting Cadoudal. They had two private interviews, in which the uncouth peasant proved much more resistant to Napoleon's fabled charm than other more polished captains. After the first meeting with this 'boorish' *gros Breton*, he remained hopeful of some progress, but Cadoudal stormed out of the second, loudly wishing he had strangled 'that little runt' (*gringolet*). Rather than help to pacify his defeated Breton chouans, he made his way to England to concoct plots with his king. But by April 1800 the west seemed calm enough for the suspension of constitutional guarantees to be lifted.

The end of politicized insurrection did not bring the end of more random disorder. Habits of brigandage did not wither with hopes of a royalist restoration. But everyday disorder was now a problem of policing rather than repression, and lack of adequate policing had bedevilled revolutionary society since the beginning. The democratization of the National Guard had made it less rather than more reliable in enforcing the law. For much of the revolutionary decade, enough troops from the regular army could not be spared from fighting foreign enemies to reinforce domestic security adequately. In any case, Napoleon believed that regular soldiers should only be used to keep internal order as a last resort. In his view, the burden of rural policing should be borne by the gendarmerie.

The gendarmerie originated in a revolutionary reorganization of the *Maréchausée*, the rural police force of the old regime (16 February 1791). A paramilitary body of partially mounted police, it had units throughout the country under an overall central command, but proved neither numerous enough nor well enough recruited or trained to stem endemic crime. Its deficiencies were recognized in a report to the post-Fructidorean councils in April 1798, resulting in a law reorganizing it into a force of 10,575 accredited former soldiers. But little had been done to implement the new structures by the time of Brumaire. Napoleon's retrospective opinion was that it was worthless. As first consul he received reports of brigands raiding traffic even heavily guarded by gendarmes, of gendarmes who fled rather than fought and squads without adequate armaments. And in these parts more than elsewhere, noted one northern commander, 'it seems to have been preferred, if I may put it this way, to staff the gendarmerie only with a bunch of brigands.'[16] As soon as relative calm was restored in the west, the consular government set about purging the force and equipping it properly. Numbers were increased to 16,000, now to be recruited exclusively from former soldiers with at least three campaigns' service. They were to be tall, literate and not natives of the area to which they were posted. Brigades of six men each, well-armed and half of them mounted, were to be evenly distributed across the country. By 1805 Napoleon was claiming that the reformed gendarmerie had enabled him to restore order in France; and the next year, he urged his brother, newly installed as king of Naples, to create such a force.[17]

> It is an organization apart which does not exist anywhere else in Europe ... It is the most effective way of maintaining the peace in a country, and keeps a half-civil, half-military watch over the whole land with the most exact reports. Do not believe that a few pickets, a few mobile detachments ... will obtain these results. You need fixed detachments that localities and individuals get to know. The only drawback is that all this is rather expensive.

Progress in rebuilding the gendarmerie was not instantaneous; but by the time of the Peace of Amiens, foreign visitors noted the presence of patrols along the main roads, which at least made them feel safe. When the future British prime minister Lord John Russell visited the fallen emperor on Elba in 1814, 'I told him that I had heard everywhere, that during his reign the robberies and pillage which had been common before, had almost ceased; he said quickly, "*C'était la gendarmerie.*"'[18]

Gendarmes were answerable in the first instance to the new supreme officer in each department, the prefect. One of the main political aspirations of 1789 had been to devolve power and rid the country of the despotic authority of the royal provincial intendants. And so, for four years, central government had had no formal direct administrative links with lower levels. The emergencies of 1793 had brought recentralization in the form of deputies with plenary powers sent on mission to disturbed areas; and then, under 'revolutionary government', the appointment of 'national agents' in every district, reporting directly to the Convention's governing committees. And although these were all temporary expedients, lapsing when the constitution of 1795 came into force, that constitution, notionally restoring representative authority at every level, also assigned a 'national commissioner' to every department and municipality. These commissioners were responsible to the Directory for the application of all laws, yet they were chosen from prominent local residents, and so subject to the same pressures and disincentives as the elected officials with whom they shared authority. But prefects, introduced by one of the earliest administrative reforms of the consulate in the law of 28 Pluviôse Year VIII/18 February 1800, shared power with nobody, nor were they generally local men. Untenured, and entirely dependent on ministers, their job was to apply and enforce all laws and decisions taken in Paris and to report regularly on their effectiveness in their departments. Individual initiative was not expected of them, but their impact was closely monitored. The first success of what would prove one of the most enduring of Napoleonic creations was the prefects' role in the steady diminution of brigandage and crime which marked the consular years.

Additionally, the machinery of justice which underpinned policy was also radically reorganized, reversing many of the Revolution's liberal reforms. The most fundamental of these had been the election of magistrates and trial by jury. Both magistracy and jury service had originally been confined to active citizens with prescribed qualifications in terms of wealth and property, but the Convention conferred eligibility on all male citizens. This opened the appointment of judges and jurors to people of little education, experience or ability, and, in the populist atmosphere of 1793–4, to rampant social and political partisanship. It was only accentuated in the seesaw years after Thermidor. It made judges reluctant to indict, and juries to convict, knowing that at the next swing of the pendulum they might themselves fall victim to politicized justice. Even when property requirements were restored under the 1795 constitution, these pressures remained, not to mention the problem of intimidation. Witnesses were often afraid to testify against defendants who knew them, while qualified candidates could be unwilling to accept service as judges, jurors or even public officials of any sort. One notorious Breton brigand, it was reported in January 1801,

> attacks the mayors and municipal officers of rural communes; he has tied some of them to planks; and trussed like this, they are cruelly beaten. It has become difficult to find officers to take these posts. Some even give them up after accepting . . . citizens seem quite disgusted by them. It is the same for justices of the peace, and it is to be presumed that these brigands wish to bring anarchy to these parts, by scaring public officials and putting them off their functions.[19]

Nor did matters improve immediately after Brumaire. Quite the reverse: the first impulse of the consulate was a mass purge of questionable magistrates and local officials, which left many positions of authority unstaffed, and cases unjudged for months over the winter of 1799–1800. But when these gaps were filled during the subsequent summer, only justices of the peace continued to be chosen by election. Higher magistrates and local government officers were now, like the prefects, nominated from above, and answerable to the state rather than to their fellow citizens. Juries, despite sustained criticism by many jurisconsults, and the open hostility of Napoleon himself, did not for the moment disappear from the regular courts; but in areas where brigandage persisted, special courts were introduced to dispense swift and summary justice by judges alone.

There were two sorts. In March 1800, hard upon the surrender of the western chouan leaders, the first consul turned his attention to the other area of notorious brigandage, the Rhône valley and the far southeast. Bands of troops and national guardsmen, organized into 'flying columns', whose effectiveness against bandits and guerrillas had been demonstrated throughout the western insurgencies, were authorized to scour disturbed southern departments, killing armed brigands out of hand and trying other captives before military commissions, judging without appeal. By no means all suspects sent before these commissions were condemned. Many got a fairer trial than they might have from a partisan jury. But several hundred brigands were sentenced to be shot. The police minister, Fouché, disliked the autonomy with which the military commissions operated; but, equally unconvinced of the efficacy of trial by jury, he became an advocate of special courts to deal with highway robbers, deserters and bandits who attacked the forces of order. The first consul ignored his pleas until the bomb plot that nearly cost him his life in December 1800. Although unwilling to accept Fouché's proof that the attack was the work of royalists and not the former Jacobins whom he was determined to blame, Napoleon was shocked into accepting the need for extraordinary courts. A decree was prepared within weeks and, despite an outburst of libertarian protest in the Tribunate, it became law on 7 February (18 Pluviôse Year IX). It empowered the government to set up special tribunals in areas it considered disturbed. Made up of two lawyers, two soldiers and two nominated citizens, they tried cases without juries and without a right of appeal against their sentences. Their brief was to try 'all crimes linked to the violent passions aroused by ten years of revolution. And bring about a situation needing time for men to be able to accustom themselves to calm and wellbeing, and to resign themselves to bear with docility the yoke of public felicity.'[20] Their existence was to be strictly temporary, until order was decreed restored, but at their height, the courts operated in 36 departments. Their capital sentences, unlike the firing squads used by military commissions, were carried out by guillotine, evoking the memory of the special tribunals of 1793–4. No wonder their activity was soon being called the 'Consular Terror'.

It was nothing like as destructive statistically as its earlier namesake but spectacular enough, and intentionally so, in the districts it targeted. Napoleon was always a firm believer in the deterrent power of vivid examples. And so, between the consolidation of his power after Marengo and the final conclusion of peace with the Church and all foreign enemies in 1802, there were between 2,000 and 2,500 executions ordered by special commissions or tribunals. Nor do these bald figures do justice to the repressive apparatus and activity of which they were the ultimate outcome. The army and the gendarmerie knew that chouans and brigands thrived on their ability to melt back in the communities where they operated. To flush them out, these refuges had to be terrorized to such an extent that the inhabitants were more afraid of the forces of order than of brigands themselves. The indiscriminate brutality of undisciplined, often underpaid and undersupplied soldiery was notorious, and their officers took no special pains to restrain them.

But over this period some of the deeper mainsprings of disorder faded away. Peace with foreign enemies brought a decline in the need for conscripts, and in May 1802 an amnesty was declared for draft evaders. A staggering 172,000 turned themselves in. Peace with the Church, promised by Napoleon to the chouan leaders even before he subdued them, was on the horizon throughout 1800 and 1801, and the faithful were increasingly allowed to worship with acceptable priests. None of these things brought a sudden or complete end to endemic criminality and brigandage, but they loosened their roots; and the steady determination of the decade of imperial rule which followed would make them looser still. Napoleon's fellow citizens, as they became his subjects, felt safer from crime and violence than they had since the collapse of the old monarchy. For too many people, the Revolution had brought more than a decade of chronic insecurity. But now, as the prefect of a western department bordering on the Vendée reported, 'the grim mistrust which when I last passed through made all the locals shun me, has given way to gentler sentiments. They like a government which protects them, and in several cottages, I have seen a sincere health drunk to the First Consul.'[21] He was not slow in claiming the credit. At the Council of State in March 1802 he boasted that 'With my prefects, my gendarmes, and my priests, I shall always do whatever I wish.'[22] But, as Chateaubriand observed as the new regime sought to resurrect pre-revolutionary ceremonial, 'this was not order, this was discipline.'[23]

James Gillray, 'Introduction of Citizen Volpone & His Suite, at Paris',
1802, etching. Gillray mocks Charles James Fox's visit to Napoleon.

6

An Experimental Peace

When the grandest monarchy in Europe collapsed, unleashing the upheavals that became the French Revolution, foreigners flocked to France to witness the unprecedented scenes for themselves. Initially they were welcomed by patriots confident in the self-evident attractions of their newly proclaimed land of liberty and equality. Most came to watch and report, but some were keen to play a more active part. In June 1790 Baron Jean-Baptiste Cloots, a Prussian subject, styling himself 'Orator of the Human Race', organized a colourful deputation of foreigners to assure the Constituent Assembly of wide international support for its reforms. And the Englishman Thomas Paine, who prided himself on having triggered the American Revolution in 1776 with his pamphlet *Common Sense*, dashed to France in November 1789 to observe the triumphs of a second Revolution in Europe itself. Back in England the following spring, he wrote *Rights of Man* to refute (and outsell) Edmund Burke's denunciatory *Reflexions on the Revolution in France*. He then crossed the Channel once more to find himself in Paris when Louis XVI made his ill-fated attempt to escape. On this occasion, he drafted a famous manifesto calling for dethronement of the king and the establishment of a republic. This was enough, when republicanism triumphed just over a year later, to win Paine the grant of French citizenship, and almost at once election to the National Convention, which had been tasked with producing a republican constitution.

A number of other well-known foreigners, including Cloots, were also offered French citizenship at the same time; but this was the high point of the Revolution's welcome to outsiders. By now France was at war with Austria and Prussia, the war was going badly, and foreigners were under increasing suspicion. After the massacres of September 1792 most were only too happy to escape from such a dangerously unpredictable and volatile country. But as the number of states at war with France expanded, even the handful who opted to stay, loudly proclaiming their solidarity with the new Republic, were viewed increasingly warily as potential enemy agents. Paine sullied his revolutionary reputation for ever by opposing the death penalty for the king, and then associating too closely with the Girondins. After the downfall of the latter, Cloots hurriedly abandoned his earlier support for them, but it was not forgotten, and by the end of 1793 both he and Paine had been expelled from the Convention and were imprisoned. Accused of involvement in a so-called 'foreign plot', the Orator of the Human Race was guillotined a few months later, and Paine only survived by what he believed to have been an administrative mistake. Meanwhile, all foreigners were now required to carry passports and be registered with their local watch committees. Spanish and British subjects were ordered to be arrested and their property confiscated. In the spring of 1794 all foreigners were expelled from Paris and towns of strategic importance. Unsurprisingly, very few now attempted to visit France, other than to seek help in overthrowing their own governments.

Draconian attitudes towards aliens softened with the end of the Terror, but so long as the Republic was at war, it remained hazardous for foreigners to venture onto its territory. Those coming from enemy states were obviously most at risk, but the number of such states steadily diminished as a result of French victories during the late 1790s. Throughout these years, the only state consistently at war with France was Great Britain, and the only British subjects who were offered a, still-cautious, welcome were Irish revolutionaries like Theobald Wolfe Tone. A handful of officially accredited British visitors accompanied Lord Malmesbury on an abortive peace mission in 1796–7, but between its failure and the Brumaire coup, France remained closed to British travellers. Yet although war between the two states continued, some easing of restrictions was visible almost as soon as Napoleon took power. The first consul wanted to make peace with what became, after the Peace of Lunéville with defeated Austria in February 1801, France's last enemy. Informal negotiations, begun at the time of Lunéville, culminated in the signature of peace preliminaries on 1 October. The talks aroused increasing excitement among rich islanders longing to see for themselves how France had been revolutionized. When news of the signature of the preliminaries broke, there was a rush to book passages across the Channel. The opulent William Beckford arrived within a week with his entourage, renting a vast empty mansion in the Faubourg Saint-Germain, ready to resume a search, discontinued since 1793, for cheap aesthetic loot. And now the first consul ordered Fouché to admit any British visitors with passports. A veritable invasion began.

* * *

DURING THE SIX months it took to turn the peace preliminaries into a definitive treaty, around 2,000 British travellers visited France. Most arrived via Calais, taking the road to Paris which had been hurriedly repaired to ease the passage of the British plenipotentiary, Marquis Cornwallis, who arrived in the French capital on 7 November. Having been received by the first consul three days later, Cornwallis spent several weeks meeting other officials before moving to Amiens to open formal negotiations. But there were already enough distinguished compatriots in Paris for him to offer them a grand dinner and night at the opera, where they were loudly applauded. The influx continued over the winter, but as the negotiations at Amiens dragged on into the spring, it slowed, and, fearing a breakdown, some British visitors began to return home. But that trickle stopped when a final treaty was signed on 27 March, and a new surge of arrivals began almost immediately. 'Foreigners from all nations,' reported the *Gazette de France* on 5 August, 'and particularly the English, are flooding, above all over the last month, into the capital. You cannot take a step in the streets ... without hearing German, Italian or English spoken. But it is quite noticeable that it is this last language which predominates.'[1] Arrivals at Calais from Dover averaged around a hundred a week that summer, and at one point the envoy Anthony Merry estimated that there were 5,000 British in Paris alone. He complained that authorizing passports for them left him little time for much else. By the time a fully accredited ambassador arrived in November in the person of Lord Whitworth, the number of his compatriots had doubled, and much of his time at the first consul's monthly reception for foreign ambassadors was taken up with presenting the more distinguished of them.

France, visitors found, was alarmingly bureaucratic. The ordinary inhabitants of the Channel ports were welcoming enough and far from the 'bloody monsters' expected by Fanny Burney when she disembarked at Calais in April 1802.[2] They were clearly delighted at the reappearance of free-spending travellers. But the visitors were at once confronted by suspicious and intrusive customs officers who ransacked their luggage. They were also required to obtain passports which only ensured safe conduct to their next destination. Mostly this was Paris, where further permits to stay had to be obtained, themselves allowing no travel beyond a close perimeter. Innkeepers demanded to see them, explaining that the police regularly checked their guest lists. While deploring an intrusive surveillance unthinkable in England, visitors appreciated the relative security of a better-policed country than they had expected. 'The traveller has nothing whatever to apprehend from highway robbers or footpads,' noted Henry Redhead Yorke, 'and this I attribute to the number of *gens d'armes*, extremely well mounted, who are continually riding along the roads to ensure the safety of travellers.'[3] Talking to their hosts, tourists found them practically unanimous in praising the consular regime for restoring order out of anarchy. On the other hand, their informants knew that, in Paris at least, police spies were everywhere, constantly alert to the slightest whisper of subversion or discontent. They were particularly active in places where the British were known to congregate. From September 1802 the daily reports of the prefecture of police devoted a special section to what the islanders were doing or saying.

From the moment of their arrival in France, foreign tourists looked out for signs of revolutionary depredations. Those who had known pre-revolutionary days at once noticed the state of the roads. Once the envy of Europe, many were now in advanced disrepair, slowing down journeys and damaging vehicles. Protected by tricolour hat cockades, which they had been advised to buy on disembarking, along their journey they noted castles and country houses burnt or shut up, abandoned, and ruinous monasteries and other religious buildings. Churches had been stripped of precious ornaments, caps of liberty had been impaled on many spires and their facades painted with revolutionary slogans or thinly obliterated proclamations of belief in Robespierre's Supreme Being. But those who passed through notoriously devout Flanders found that even damaged village churches were well attended. Arriving in the month of the formal promulgation of the concordat, one Sunday, Fanny Burney 'saw, in almost all the villages, neat and clean peasants, going to, or coming from Mass, and seemingly elated and happy indescribably by the public permission of divine worship on its originally appointed Day'.[4] She was not alone in noting that the ten-day republican week was largely ignored by everybody except public officials. The concordat might continue to be a source of bitter conflict among the clergy, but with the ordinary populace of Flanders, at least, it was clearly a success. Sunday, 'two good old women' told Burney, 'was the happiest day . . . of their lives; that they had ALL lost *le bon Dieu* for these last ten years, but that Buonaparte had now found him.'[5]

Passing in ostentatious comfort through once-prosperous textile towns like Abbeville or Amiens, British travellers were repeatedly mobbed by crowds of beggars. It was enough to warn them that their hopes of a new commercial treaty allowing British manufactures into France were unlikely to be realized. Arriving in Paris, some thought that beggars were fewer than before the Revolution, but there were still over 80,000 paupers in the capital. 'These poor devils', noted the German musician Johann Friedrich Reichardt,

> do not call to you with insolence; they beg for charity in moving tones and lamentations; all the more so as, among them, there are many young men crippled in the wars . . . beggars in rags, when you give to one of them, follow you with pleas and groans . . . rushing on foreigners from all sides.[6]

Their plight was made worse over the coldest winter since 1795, as the capital was also swept by a deadly influenza epidemic. If Paris, observed Francis Blagdon, who had known it before 1789, 'affords a thousand enjoyments to the men of fortune, it may truly be said that, without money, Paris is the most melancholy abode in the world.'[7]

But visitors taking advantage of the peace did have money, and they came to Paris determined to spend it. There were innumerable coffee houses, several parks and pleasure gardens where public dancing was all the rage, not to mention the Palais Royal. No longer the hotbed of political agitation, which had made it notorious throughout the Revolution, it was once again the centre of drinking, gambling and prostitution that it had been in the 1780s, though now with a more louche clientele. No tourist failed to visit it to experience delicious horror. More respectable entertainment was available in theatres and concert halls, encouraged and regularly patronized by the first consul himself and his entourage. There was also the Louvre, now replete with the plunder of Italy. Entry was free, but, as Yorke recorded, it was a 'Gallery containing the spoils of nations, and nearly every picture bears at the bottom an inscription declaring it to be a stolen article'.[8] Equally shocking were the relics of what the revolutionaries had destroyed. There was the site of the Bastille, now housing a wood yard. There were the weed-infested mansions of the old nobility in the formerly glittering Faubourg Saint-Germain, now standing empty or reduced to collections of tenements. And there was further scope for horror in visiting Versailles. 'Once', as the Warwickshire gentleman Bertie Greatheed put it, 'the gay, the proud, the brilliant; now a desolation . . . bad as it was who can look on it in its recent nakedness without melancholy reflections on the vicissitudes of human affairs?'[9] His party lunched at a restaurant, now established in the shabbily maintained Petit Trianon. For all their wealth, the British had a reputation for meanness and were easily outspent by Russians, among whom only the very richest could have afforded to travel this far. They were more at home than most of the British (concerned, as Reichardt noted, for their respectability[10]) among the showy and vulgar enriched profiteers from the new regime who now seemed to dominate Parisian society as the old nobility once had. Not that old nobles had disappeared. Private liveries and coats of arms were no longer in evidence, and even *ci-devants* who had not lost everything kept a low profile. But they knew that the consular regime wanted to reconcile them, and most sought to requite its indulgence and discreetly rebuild their ravaged fortunes. Much more noticeable were returned émigrés, encouraged not only by the peace, but by the closure of the émigrés list a month after its final signature (20 April 1802). It was among them that some of the haughty ways and attitudes of pre-revolutionary times survived, but the police kept a particular watch on them for the least sign of sympathy for the still-exiled Bourbons.

Another group closely watched by the now-ubiquitous police were grumbling former soldiers reduced to half-pay and idleness by the diminished military requirements of continental peace. Napoleon knew that discontented soldiers, even disbanded ones, were a threat to any government. Most notorious among them was Moreau, the real winner of the war against Austria. Refusing to wear his general's uniform, he paid no court to the commander-in-chief. He boycotted the great Easter celebration of peace and the concordat on 18 April 1802, preferring to stroll, ostentatiously smoking, around the Tuileries gardens. His detachment was notorious, and foreign visitors looked out for him. They were all much keener, however, to see the peacemaker himself, if they saw nothing else in Paris. The more distinguished ones could hope to be presented to the first consul in person by their ambassador. The rest could only hope to glimpse him at the fortnightly review of troops which was now a central element in the capital's calendar. Paris was heavily garrisoned; soldiers were far more visible than before 1789 and held in much more respect. On review days they paraded in front of the Tuileries Palace. At a climactic moment the first consul would appear, simply dressed amid an entourage of gaudily uniformed generals. 'The review really consists', wrote Yorke, 'in the first consul, his generals, his aides-de-camp and his Mamelukes, trotting very fast through the lines.[11] He then takes his station in front of the gates of the Tuileries, and the troops pass him in quick time, afterwards filing off to their respective quarters.' Yorke was slightly disappointed, but several of his fellow British spectators were bowled over by the spectacle. 'By God,' exclaimed one, 'this man deserves to govern the world.' Another thing that impressed foreign onlookers was that, before returning to the palace, the head of state stood to receive petitions from the crowds. 'I must respond to them all,' he told a family friend. 'When order is beginning to be restored is not the moment I can overlook any needs or claims.'[12]

It was one of the few open public gestures from a ruler now seen to be retreating rapidly from republicanism. Increasingly, he spent time outside the capital in the Palace of Saint-Cloud, the scene of his initial seizure of power, coming to the Tuileries only for reviews and grand receptions. The military reviews were normally followed by an audience inside the palace, where the surrounding and ceremonial were all grandly monarchical. The first consul strode to and from the parades through a series of crowded antechambers in order of exclusiveness. In the final room, flanked by the two other consuls, he received distinguished visitors, foreign ambassadors and the compatriots they deemed worthy of presentation. During the early stages of the peace, before its final ratification at Amiens, he was particularly welcoming to the British. 'I am charmed', he told one party, 'to see so many English here. I hope that our union will be long lasting. We are the two most powerful and civilized nations in Europe. We must come together to cultivate the arts, sciences, letters, in fact to benefit the human race.'[13] This benign show lasted until some months after the final signature at Amiens. It culminated late in August 1802 when the great Whig parliamentarian Charles James Fox arrived in Paris, ostensibly to gather materials for a book on the Stuarts, but just as much to inspect the results of the peace which he had so long advocated against the obduracy of Pitt, and hoping against hope that the first consul was not the military despot he suspected. When, some days after arriving, he was presented, and had what he called a 'long talk with Bony', his worst fears were confirmed.[14] Napoleon set out to charm and flatter him. He had, he said, long admired Fox's oratory and his advocacy of peace. But when he began to vaut the necessity of a large standing army, Fox contradicted him, to his evident irritation. During a second meeting, the first consul broached a subject that was already becoming an obsession with him. Why was the English press allowed to insult and malign him? Fox blandly replied that in England the press was free, and people shrugged off its attacks. And when Napoleon denounced Pitt as the sponsor of the infernal machine that had nearly killed him in 1800, Fox felt obliged to defend his lifelong nemesis with a rebuttal. Returning home disillusioned, he nevertheless persisted in believing that the autocratic Napoleon saw more to be gained from maintaining the newly concluded peace than breaking it.

For the moment he did; but he also seemed increasingly ready to provoke British suspicions. On the very day Fox arrived in France, British newspapers were banned in Paris. A few days earlier a bitter article in the official *Moniteur*, widely believed to be by the first consul himself, complained that the British government had done nothing to silence their defence of 'public and private crimes'.[15] Hopes for a new commercial treaty were the talk of British visitors in Paris, and throughout the period of peace, London's representatives there were under instructions to press for one. Napoleon was not interested. He was, reminisced his interior minister, Jean-Antoine Chaptal, 'the enemy of all commercial treaties'.[16] Like so many of his compatriots, he remembered an Anglo-French commercial treaty of 1786 as a disaster for French industries, and he left all revolutionary tariffs against British imports in place, insisting that his satellite states follow France's example. His brother Joseph had reassured the people of Amiens in the spring of 1802 that there would be no new commercial treaty with the British, and later in the summer a lavish exhibition of French industrial products was mounted at the Louvre and favoured by a lengthy visit from the first consul.[17] The clear message was that France had no need of British manufactures – even though contraband goods were known to be flooding in via third countries to sate a fashion for all things English currently sweeping the capital.

Even if flattered by the fashion, the British would not have been wrong to see the exhibition, and consular refusal to discuss any sort of commercial agreement, as a challenge, if not a threat. Similarly with the first consul's departure, at the end of October, for an extended tour of Normandy and the Channel coast. The last time he had done this was to assess the prospects for an invasion in 1798. What could only be invasion barges had been noticed by the Devonshire squire Sir John Carr when he landed at Le Havre in April 1802.[18] The first consul's return from the tour seemed timed to coincide with the final arrival of the fully accredited British ambassador Lord Whitworth, who presented his credentials on 5 December.

Whitworth's mission was destined to last barely six months. He did not need veiled threats for him to arrive full of suspicion. His previous posting had been in St Petersburg, where he was believed to have been involved in the assassination of France's ally Paul I in March 1801. Napoleon's way of conducting business, he told Foreign Secretary Hawkesbury, reminded him of the late mad czar.[19] In any case, despite the apparent affability of Hawkesbury's counterpart, Talleyrand, Whitworth had no trust in anything French, and his instructions too were suffused with suspicion as to what the first consul intended. It was true that Napoleon's first attempt to profit from peace on the seas was now coming apart. Having met with some initial success, the massive amphibious expedition sent the year before to recover control of Saint-Domingue and other Caribbean islands was now facing defeat at the hands of former slaves and decimation by yellow fever. In January 1803 it was learnt that its commander, Napoleon's own brother-in-law Charles Victor Emmanuel Leclerc, had himself succumbed to the disease.[20] There was much British gloating as this debacle unfolded, but worry too that its failure might divert ambitions back towards the Mediterranean. The French commitment at Amiens to remove troops occupying the southern ports of the Neapolitan kingdom, obvious departure points for the Levant, had not yet been honoured. And in August 1802 Colonel Horace Sébastiani had been dispatched on a tour of the eastern Mediterranean to assess the probabilities of recovering Egypt. When he returned in January 1803 his report to the first consul was immediately published in the *Moniteur*. It declared that Egypt could easily be recaptured by a force of 10,000 troops. This, not to mention his exotic bodyguard of Mamelukes, made plain to the British that Napoleon was not reconciled to the loss of conquests he had abandoned in 1799. It came at the very moment when the British government had decided to withdraw its own remaining victorious troops from Egypt. It made them all the more determined not to evacuate Malta. Hawkesbury scarcely needed Whitworth's advice that

> from the moment that Malta is under the influence of France – which it must be from the moment His Majesty's troops are withdrawn – we can no longer depend on the preservation of peace on any terms with this country, supposing that the occupation of Egypt by France is to be resisted.[21]

The status of Malta had already proved the thorniest issue in all the negotiations at Amiens; and although the British had agreed in principle to evacuate, the precise circumstances envisaged for their departure were full of ambiguities, providing ample pretexts for delay. More than anything else this was the issue on which the Peace of Amiens would founder.

But it was not the only threat to the experimental peace. Having agreed to give up most of their wartime gains, the British had hoped that France would reciprocate by not attempting to extend its already dominant continental influence. They had hoped that a peace signed simultaneously with the Dutch would lead to the withdrawal of French troops from the Batavian Republic, already promised in the Peace of Lunéville. They were not withdrawn, and France continued to dictate the course of Dutch politics. Switzerland, from which the British had co-ordinated counter-revolutionary plots throughout the 1790s, was another source of concern. Although now a sister republic, it was torn by factions, some of whom openly sought British support. Napoleon was now tired, he told Talleyrand, of these 'childish games'.[22] 'It is time for this to end ... and I see nothing between a Swiss government solidly organized and friendly to France, or no Switzerland.' Even as Whitworth arrived in France, French troops were invading the sister republic to stifle the instability. By then, too, in September France had formally annexed Piedmont. The former heartland of the Savoyard monarchy had been under French occupation since 1800, but its notional independence had been respected as a sop to the monarchical sensitivities of Czar Paul I. But as soon as assassination had removed this volatile ally from the diplomatic equation, a process of rapidly absorbing Piedmont into France was begun. It was perhaps scarcely a surprise, but it came in the wake of a further consolidation of French power in Italy where the Cisalpine Republic first created by Napoleon in 1797 had been recreated with expanded frontiers. At a grand and carefully orchestrated conference, or *consulta*, of Lombard notables held at Lyon in January 1802, the restored puppet state was proclaimed the Italian Republic, and Napoleon its president. It took place while the final negotiation of the Peace of Amiens was in progress.

All this reflected the first consul's view that nothing on the continent was any of Britain's business; and despite British anxieties, Italy was not mentioned in the final treaty. But the British, for their part, never accepted exclusion from continental affairs, and when, during the fallout from Sébastiani's report, Talleyrand, speaking with his master's voice, enquired of Whitworth what progress was being made in the evacuation of Malta, he was told that in view of the steady expansion of France's power, and particularly the annexation of Piedmont, Britain was seeking compensation by delaying implementation of its own side of the Amiens accords. Hawkesbury took the same stance with the French ambassador in London, General Antoine François Andréossy. Surprised, perhaps, by this sudden intransigence, on 18 February Napoleon summoned Whitworth to a private meeting at the Tuileries. There he harangued the stiff ambassador for two hours, jumping from topic to topic and scarcely allowing any opportunity for a response. 'His purpose', Whitworth reported, 'was evidently to convince me that on Malta must depend peace or war, and at the same time to impress upon my mind a strong idea of the means he possessed of annoying us at home and abroad.'[23] He could, Napoleon asserted, take Egypt whenever he liked, but predicted that sooner or later it would fall to France anyway. And however hazardous the prospect, he claimed to be also strong enough to attempt an invasion of England directly. His advances in Switzerland and Piedmont, on the other hand, were no cause for alarm, mere trifles: 'the expression he made use of', Whitworth observed, 'was too trivial and vulgar to find a place in a despatch, or anywhere but in the mouth of a hackney coachman.'[24] And meanwhile he complained of the way London tolerated the activities of the Bourbons and their supporters like Cadoudal, and the outrageous treatment he and his family continued to receive from the press in Britain, both native papers and those of French exiles.

While constantly protesting that, in pointed contrast to France, the press in Britain was free, the British government had made one gesture to meet Napoleon's complaints. In September 1802, after sustained diplomatic pressure, a prosecution for criminal libel was launched against one of the more prominent French émigré journalists, Jean-Gabriel Peltier. He was accused of inciting his compatriots, in a French-language newspaper published in London, to assassinate the first consul and restore the Bourbons.

The case came to court on 21 February 1803 at the very moment when Napoleon was attempting to browbeat Whitworth. At the direction of the judge, Peltier lost; but sentencing was postponed and he used the delay to publish and sell his own version of the trial in both English and French. So far from silencing him, the trial made Peltier a celebrity, and even the Paris police reported that English visitors in the city spoke of nothing else. And so far from deterring further attacks on the first consul in the London press, the case only encouraged them. Whitworth was increasingly alarmed at their impact. That, as well as hardening British intransigence over Malta and news that the London government had just announced plans to recruit 10,000 sailors and embody the militia, was the spur to Napoleon's next assault on the ambassador at a diplomatic reception on 13 March. In the presence of all the other major ambassadors and a number of British visitors hoping for presentation by Whitworth, the first consul declared that, if necessary, he would fight the British for another fifteen years. 'What can we do', he said on turning to the Russian ambassador, 'if they don't wish to keep to the treaty?' Later he returned to Whitworth, clearly agitated. 'If the storm must break,' he shouted, 'if there must be great revenge, the fault before God and mankind will lie with those who have not wished to execute the treaty of Amiens. If you take up arms we shall arm too!' 'While he stood talking,' observed a British eyewitness, 'his eyes roved about the room, he rolled from leg to leg and gave threatening shakes of his head' before stalking out.[25] With several hundred spectators in the room, this undiplomatic outburst caused a sensation. Soon the whole city knew about it. Whitworth at once shared his aristocratic disdain for such vulgar histrionics with Talleyrand, who was clearly sympathetic when the ambassador said he could not attend another consular reception unless he could rely on better manners. And, in fact, he only ever met Napoleon briefly once again. The word 'war' had now been publicly uttered by the first consul, and soon British visitors began to leave Paris. Bets were being placed in London on how soon fighting would begin. Negotiations did indeed continue until early May as Talleyrand at least, now abetted by Joseph Bonaparte as one of the signatories of the Amiens treaty, attempted to play for time. But British attitudes were hardening further. The French 'must be convinced', Whitworth wrote to an approving Hawkesbury, 'that the question is – Malta or war.'[26]

Both sides were now mobilizing. The measures announced in London early in March were taking effect. Having previously denied fortification of the Channel coasts which had allegedly provoked these steps, the French began openly reinforcing them and assembling an invasion fleet. On 26 April two whole classes of conscripts, numbering 60,000, were called up. The government advised French merchants not to put to sea and British visitors were forbidden to leave the Republic except via Calais or Boulogne – presumably to prevent them reporting on naval and military preparations. Meanwhile, diplomatic exchanges were deadlocked, and on 1 May Whitworth presented a formal ultimatum. In exchange for recognizing the consolidation of French power in Italy, France must accept British occupation of Malta and evacuate her own troops from Holland and Switzerland. In the event of a refusal, the ambassador was instructed to return to England. As Hawkesbury must have expected, the demands were rejected. There should be no more blathering (*parlage*), the first consul instructed his foreign secretary.[27] If this was an ultimatum, a word threatening war, let the ambassador say so: 'we are tired of this state of anxiety.' 'Show yourself cold, lofty, and even somewhat proud . . . scare him.' But Whitworth was not easily scared. He calmly asked for his passport and headed for Calais. Even as he journeyed, the French made a last-minute offer to allow the British to remain in Malta for ten years; but nothing was said about troop withdrawals from Holland or Switzerland. Hawkesbury was no longer interested. The Peace of Amiens was over.

Throughout his despatches to London, Whitworth emphasized how difficult Napoleon was to control. He had the impression
that his brother Joseph and Talleyrand were constantly striving
to restrain his aggressive impulses. So was the Second Consul
Cambacérès, who, looking back in his memoirs, deplored the
way that Napoleon 'allowed himself to be carried away by resentment, and by an argumentative bent that he could never resist'.[28]
His resentful instincts were now deployed to the full. The British
government did not wait for Whitworth's return on 20 May to
begin hostilities. Four days before, it had ordered the Royal Navy
to attack and detain French shipping. A declaration of war came
on 18 May. Napoleon's response was to authorize the same action
against British shipping by both regular forces and privateers: but
also to decree the arrest of all British subjects in France between
the ages of eighteen and sixty, deeming them prisoners of war.
The pretext was that, technically liable for militia service, they
were members of the enemy's armed forces. The second consul
himself was horrified at an act that he told Napoleon looked like
'unprecedented tyranny, and which besides can produce no real
advantage. Your reputation could be damaged.'[29] It certainly was;
but the first consul's vengeful fury was not to be assuaged. It was
more shocking for being unexpected. Even as the war clouds gath-
ered, *The Argus*, an English-language newspaper produced in Paris
by the consular government, was assuring its readers that British
passport holders were safe, whatever happened. Even as late as the
first week in May, some British visitors were still arriving. Many
more, however, were preparing to leave, and when Whitworth did
so, there was a rush for the Channel and some very narrow escapes.
The government claimed that 7,500 were 'detained', although later
counts have reduced this to seven hundred. But most of these, if
they survived, never saw their native land again until 1814.

* * *

THERE WAS, HOWEVER, one Englishman in Paris for whom the peace had brought a longed-for opportunity to get out. On 1 September 1802 Thomas Paine, the international revolutionary, after ten years' residence in the world capital of revolution, set sail from Le Havre for America. For British tourists until then, Paine was one of the minor sights of Paris. He was, after all, though now an American and a French citizen, their most notorious compatriot. After failing to save Louis XVI from the guillotine, he had vowed to leave the country, but having evaded trial in England on sedition charges he could scarcely return there, and in any case only weeks after his pleas for the king's life, the French Republic declared war on Great Britain. In British terms this made Paine an enemy alien at best, a traitor at worst. And now the risk of returning to America on seas dominated by the Royal Navy was too great. He was marooned in France.

It was to prove a decade of tribulation. He spent ten months in prison and emerged late in 1794 resentful that his old friend George Washington, now president of the United States, had not done more to secure his earlier release. Disgusted by the trend of politics, he spent his time behind bars writing a fierce denunciation of Christianity and the Bible: *The Age of Reason*. It went down well enough in a republic now renouncing all religious affiliation. He could even feel vindicated by the Directorial support given in 1797–8 to the deistic cult of Theophilanthropy. But in the English-speaking world the book proved disastrous for his reputation. Whereas in conservative circles it merely reinforced his notoriety as the enemy of all good order, radicals who had been his staunch supporters were often committed Christians, and on both sides of the Atlantic they were dismayed to find their champion so scornful of the Bible.

Until the coup of Fructidor, Paine despised the Directory as a betrayal of revolutionary ideals. He was then cheered, however, by news of mutinies and financial panics in Great Britain and was delighted when the Republic's most successful general, returning victorious from Italy, was appointed to command an army to invade England. Even more so, when Bonaparte sought his advice, inviting him to dinner and declaring that he slept with *Rights of Man* under his pillow.[30] Paine appears to have convinced the young general that most English people were anxious to throw off rulers who did not speak for them – a view which, according to Cambacérès, Napoleon never abandoned.[31] But Paine told him that the only sure way to defeat the British was to destroy their commerce, which would be the work of time. It was advice that, as emperor, Napoleon would follow a few years later, but now he found it unwelcome. It was yet another disappointment, both to Paine and the United Irish exiles who were now his chief drinking companions, when the hero of Italy sailed off to Egypt at the very moment when a pro-French rebellion broke out in Ireland. His return from Egypt, and subsequent seizure of power, completed Paine's disillusionment. By the time Henry Redhead Yorke visited the self-styled 'citizen of the world' early in 1802, he said he detested and despised Bonaparte, declaring that he was 'the completest charlatan that ever existed'.[32] 'No honest man', he said, 'should live in this country, they do not and cannot understand the principles of free government. They have conquered half Europe only to make it more miserable than before.' When Yorke mentioned the Republic, 'Republic!' he exclaimed, 'this is no Republic! I know of no Republic but that of America, and that is the only place for men like you and I. It is my intention to return as soon as possible . . . For myself I renounce all European politics.'[33]

But even American politics were forbidden him. In April 1800 he was threatened with deportation if he continued to pester American diplomats. He took his usual solace in the bottle, and in preparing further polemics against Christianity, but now found the consulate reconciled with the despised Catholic Church and withdrawing recognition from Theophilanthropy. The chance of election, however, in 1801 brought his old friend Thomas Jefferson to the presidency of the United States. He invited the author of *Common Sense* to return to America, promising him a warm welcome. When peace with the British made the seas safe again, Paine eagerly accepted. His welcome across the Atlantic was indeed warm, but hardly in the way Jefferson had led him to expect in that God-fearing republic.[34] Yet the moment was symbolically appropriate. The great revolutionary was leaving behind a country where the Revolution he had hailed with such enthusiasm thirteen years earlier was now over and done with.

Conclusion

As the proud prophet of one successful revolution, in the early 1790s, Thomas Paine had shared the boundless optimism of the men who had set out to forge another in the heart of Europe. But in brushing aside the gloomy predictions of Edmund Burke, his *Rights of Man* had never addressed the most prescient of all the Irishman's reflections: that in the end,

> some popular general, who understands the art of conciliating the soldiery, and who possesses the true spirit of command, shall draw the eyes of all men upon himself. Armies will obey him on his personal account ... the moment in which that event shall happen, the person who really commands the army is your master ... the master of your whole republic.

Burke was dead by the time it happened, but Paine, marooned in France, was there to witness the steady crumbling of his republican dreams and the final triumph of a general. He had believed that republics did not make war, but although it had not been a republic which launched the revolutionary wars in 1792, by the time the French forces began to achieve victories it was in a republic's name that they triumphed. They then spent the best part of two years fighting to ensure its very survival, endowing it in the process with what no regime since July 1789 had been able to rely on – a large and disciplined army. However flawed Paine thought the Republic that emerged after the Terror, he could only applaud when, in 1795 and again in 1797, troops were deployed domestically to save it from royalists or their fellow travellers. On both occasions Bonaparte was the general giving the orders. Flattered by his attentions, for a time Paine hoped that the Republic's saviour, the hero who had republicanized northern Italy, would belatedly carry the blessings of French liberty to the British Isles. No such illusions were left when the Corsican adventurer returned from Egypt. He now deployed his military prestige to steadily eviscerate the Republic, expunging any doubts lingering from his ambiguous adventures in the East by his triumph at Marengo and subsequent peace with victory against all of France's enemies. By the time Paine embarked for America, the first consul had already achieved tenure for life and the right to name his own successor. He was already a monarch, and within two more years would finally place a crown on his own head. And, as the overwhelming result of the 'constitutional vote' which followed made clear, a return to monarchy was what the political nation wanted.[1]

The French Revolution's republican experiment had not been a success. If, as Paine defined it, republicanism meant 'government by election and representation', it had repeatedly failed. It had been less than a year before the first legislature elected under the Constitution of the Year III was purged, and every subsequent election had been rigged, whether in advance or after the results were in. The Republic had not been without impressive achievements, but Bonaparte's claims to power were based upon denigrating or minimizing them. Meanwhile he and his supporters repeatedly emphasized how they were solving the problems that had defeated successive republican regimes. The memory of Terror, and fear of its return, had never been fully exorcized. It had not been forgotten that an elected Convention had suspended its own constitution, then authorized and connived at a system of repression justified by ferocious egalitarian rhetoric. The Constitution of the Year III, so unworkable, had been the creation of this same body. The memory of its terroristic beginnings would sully the reputation of French and, indeed, all European republicanism for almost a century, and in 1799 the grisly memory was all too fresh.

Something like a Jacobin resurgence, with renewed talk of emergency government and penal legislation, had marked the months before Bonaparte's return from Egypt; and the coup of Brumaire was dressed up as saving the Republic from a Jacobin conspiracy. The implicit promise of France's new ruler was that there would be no return to the Terror associated with Jacobin rule. Nor was there: but the consulate consolidated itself with terror of its own, in which thousands died. And France under Napoleon, though constantly vaunting the rule of law, would always be a police state. By 1810 the state prisons of the empire housed almost 30,000 inmates, and a number of new ones were being constructed. Napoleon's version of terror, however, would be reassuringly justified in terms of keeping social order, with none of the inflammatory democratic rhetoric used to vindicate repression in the Year II.

And apart from the flawed facade of the plebiscites of 1800, 1802 and 1804, there was nothing democratic about consular reorganization of the post-revolutionary state. The two legislative chambers, and the Senate, were made up of nominees, not elected representatives. In 1802 both the chambers were shamelessly purged to eliminate critics of the regime. Election of public officials was abandoned at every important level, meeting no serious resistance. Nowhere was the claim of 1799, that the Revolution was established on the principles with which it began, more blatantly flouted. Power was ruthlessly centralized, but as Sieyès had hoped, it seemed that a restoration of authority from above bred confidence from below.

Nothing did more to foster that confidence than resolution of the religious question. Many of the reforms and innovations of the consulate had been fairly consensual among the Brumairians who supported or welcomed the general's seizure of power. Sometimes half-formulated already, like the Civil Code, they only awaited a strong and determined authority to bring them to fruition. But the concordat with the papacy was largely the first consul's own project. It was pushed through by him in the face of widespread opposition among these same Brumairians, not to mention the army whose support mattered to him even more. These battle-scarred survivors knew that refractory priests, encouraged by Roman intransigence, had been the Republic's most persistent and pernicious enemies. They genuinely thought that the wisest course lay in the total disengagement from all religious affiliations proclaimed in 1795. Apart from tolerating all creeds – also a natural corollary of disengagement – this had not been the Revolution's original religious project. But by the time the Republic was established, the original Civil Constitution of the Clergy was already a virtual dead letter, and within a year the Convention was countenancing complete dechristianization. To reintroduce any sort of official recognition for organized religion, let alone through a deal with the pope, seemed like a betrayal of what the Revolution had become. So it was. But Napoleon recognized that a majority of the French had never accepted the loss of priests and religious observance; and he saw, too, that this loss had been the most fertile seedbed of counter-revolution and loyalty to the Bourbons. And, from his experience in Italy in 1796–7, he knew that only a deal with the pope could make a credible peace with the Church. Stripped, like everything else in the consular state, of all traces of election, the concordat of 1801 looked otherwise very like the Civil Constitution of 1790 and was predicated in the same way on the loss of the Church's independent wealth. But unlike the Civil Constitution, it was concerted with the pope, and that gave it doctrinal legitimacy. It proved far from restoring immediate peace among the clergy, and very soon amicable relations between Pius VII and Emperor Napoleon would begin to break down. But regular and unimpeded religious observance among the laity had been firmly re-established and would go on largely undisturbed by persistent quarrels between clerics or high-level clashes between pope and emperor. The deepest divide opened up by the Revolution had been, if not completely closed up, at least bridged.

On 14 July 1802, the thirteenth anniversary of the fall of the Bastille, there were lavish celebrations and a grand military parade in Paris at which the first consul took the salute. He issued a proud proclamation, praising his fellow citizens for having 'overcome all obstacles and accomplished their destiny'.[2] A year later, the atmosphere was very different. Napoleon was away, inspecting fortifications in Belgium. And in Paris, the English visitor Bertie Greatheed observed, 'This day of commemoration is dying away apace ... the concourse of people was great but by no means what I expected. The bridges, the wings of the Thuileries were not illuminated as on former occasions; there were no fireworks; no music. The night was windy and gloomy.'[3] Evidently it was scarcely any longer worth commemorating the founding event of the Revolution, because the Revolution was over. The regime still flew the tricolour, as it would until the end, but even before the triumphant Bastille Day of 1802, it was noticed that it had begun to be embroidered with the words *Empire français.*[4]

Napoleon was exultant and optimistic about the future. He was at war again, which he loved. The Revolution might have transformed the country, and opened his path to power, but it was behind him. 'When I was young,' he told the Austrian ambassador Klemens von Metternich, 'I was revolutionary from ignorance and ambition. At the age of reason, I have followed its counsels and my own instinct, and I have crushed the Revolution.'[5]

Anonymous, 'Toussaint Louverture, Leader of the Insurgent Blacks of Saint-Domingue', *c.* 1800, engraving.

Epilogue:
Cutting Overseas Losses

Peace on the seas opened the way to confronting the Revolution's colonial legacies. There is no evidence of what the young Napoleon may have thought about colonial questions, although he can scarcely have been unaware throughout the 1790s that the French islands in the Caribbean were in turmoil. He must have learnt something about the pre-revolutionary situation in Martinique from Joséphine, who was born there and only left at the age of fifteen. But, as his arguments of 1797 for striking at British India via Egypt show, he recognized even before becoming first consul how much a state's power could be boosted by colonial wealth.

Pre-revolutionary France had had its own outposts in India and in tropical islands east of the Cape, but the powerhouse of its overseas economy was in the West Indies. Here the French empire consisted of eight islands, the outpost of Guiana on the mainland of South America and, above all, the western half of Hispaniola, Saint-Domingue, the 'Pearl of the Antilles'. In 1789 this colony alone supplied most of continental Europe's limitless appetite for sugar and coffee and was recognized as the most valuable piece of territory in the world. West Indian products underpinned the booming prosperity of the ports of France's Atlantic seaboard, such as Bordeaux, Nantes and Le Havre – all of it based ultimately on the labours of black slaves. There were almost half a million of them in Saint-Domingue alone. Fear of often-predicted slave uprisings haunted the 40,000 whites and 30,000 mixed-race people who dominated society in the colony, and the initial impact of the Revolution was to provoke rivalry between these groups, as the whites sought to exclude free people of mixed race from the newly proclaimed rights of man and the citizen. Absentee plantation owners formed a powerful white lobby in France, resisting all attempts in the National Assembly to extend political rights in the colonies. But coloured resentment of exclusion in Saint-Domingue led to increasingly violent clashes, which reinforcing the garrison did little to contain. Eventually the fragmentation of social and political authority opened the way in August 1791 to the long-dreaded slave insurrection. It brought devastation to hundreds of plantations in the colony's fertile northern plains, and widespread massacres of both white and mixed-race slave owners.

It took several months for the impact to be felt in France, but by January 1792 shortages of sugar and coffee were leading to disturbances in Paris. Special commissioners were dispatched by the Legislative Assembly to restore order in the colony, but by then war had broken out in Europe, and no extra troops could be spared to reinforce their authority. When war was also declared on the British in January 1793, communication with all the overseas colonies became uncertain. The commissioners were obliged to bolster their authority by seeking alliances among shifting local factions, and by the summer they had reached the conclusion that the only way to win over a solid base of support was to offer slaves their freedom. This radical gesture was not authorized from France, but once made it was irrevocable. The Convention was persuaded that there was no alternative to recognizing and building on a fait accompli. In February 1794 slavery was formally abolished throughout French overseas territories.

Never before in history had a state committed itself to abolishing slavery. But the decree was concocted in a hurry and passed in a thin house. What made the question so urgent was the need for the Republic to confront the great maritime enemy. Throughout the eighteenth century British seapower had always been able to imperil links between France and her colonies when war broke out. But now it offered hope to beleaguered white planters. There had also been slave uprisings in Martinique and Guadeloupe, and appeals went out from white planters in all three territories for British forces to come to their rescue. The potential spoils for the British were irresistible, and in September 1793 they began to land troops in Saint-Domingue. It was partly to meet this expected invasion, and the revived white resistance that it promised to inspire, that slave emancipation was first proclaimed by the desperate commissioners, now representing the Republic. In the spring of 1794 British expeditions also took Martinique and Guadeloupe, just before news arrived from France of general emancipation. Thus the decree never took effect in Martinique, where the British kept slavery in being. Guadeloupe, however, was soon recaptured by a relief expedition. Sent by the Jacobin Convention, it used the terroristic methods then prevalent in France to eliminate the white planters who had welcomed the British and proclaimed the slave emancipation that was now the Republic's policy. In the sparsely populated enclave of Guiana the decree had taken effect without difficulty, whereas planters in the Indian Ocean islands simply refused to recognize it. In Saint-Domingue, however, it transformed the situation, bringing together most of the black population to resist the British invaders.

It took five years to expel them, even though their forces were ravaged by tropical diseases. Throughout that time the struggle was impeded by constant clashes between rival armed factions whose only common commitment was hostility to slavery. But by the time the British withdrew in 1798 a dominant native leader had emerged in the person of the former slave Pierre-Dominique Toussaint Louverture. Commanding a largely black army, he was able to reduce a succession of envoys from France to impotence – including general Hédouville, who later went on to confront the chouans. Despite this, Toussaint proclaimed himself a loyal French republican. When news arrived of the regime change in France at the end of 1799, he wrote to the first consul professing his commitment. He received no reply; but was perhaps encouraged by a consular proclamation of 25 December 1799 addressed to the 'Brave Blacks' of Saint-Domingue. It declared that 'the sacred principles of liberty and equality of black men will never be tainted or modified among you.'[1] Yet it is not clear how much thought France's new ruler gave to colonial matters until he established peace in Europe. He appears to have accepted that Toussaint offered the best hope of keeping order in Saint-Domingue. Without black soldiers, he observed in August 1800, the colony would have been lost, and they had been loyal because they were free. 'And so, I shall talk of freedom in the free part of Saint-Domingue [while] re-establishing order and introducing discipline.'[2] But he added, ominously, that he would keep slavery in the Indian Ocean colonies, and also in the Spanish half of the island, which had been ceded to France in 1795 but not yet taken over.

In this, however, Toussaint had pre-empted him. On his own initiative, but in the name of the Republic, in January 1801 he invaded the neighbouring territory and proclaimed slave emancipation there. He then proceeded to draft a new constitution for the whole united island. It acknowledged that Saint-Domingue remained part of the French empire and subject to revolutionary laws – which of course included the abolition of slavery. But it also proclaimed Toussaint governor for life. It was not quite a declaration of independence, but from France it looked like one, and the first consul was not prepared to tolerate the sort of independent insubordination that he himself had displayed in Italy five years earlier. Plans had been laid as early as January 1800 for a military expedition to reassert metropolitan authority in the Caribbean but had been called off for fear of interception by the Royal Navy. By the summer of 1801, however, the British were negotiating peace preliminaries, and the prospect of unimpeded Atlantic crossings revived the project. Within a week of the signature of formal preliminaries in October, a vast amphibious operation began to be assembled, comprising around one hundred ships and 20,000 seasoned soldiers. The intention was clear: to recover control of Saint-Domingue with a view to recreating the commercial prosperity, which the slave rebellion and the war at sea had destroyed.

The first consul's brother-in-law, the general Charles Leclerc, was given command. He was instructed to proceed gently until full military control had been established. A flattering letter was sent to Toussaint, asking for his co-operation, even as it declared that his new constitution was unacceptable. The first consul promised to maintain the abolition of slavery, even though by this time he was privately declaring that, as a white man, he was against black people and did not wish to see them given any superior power or authority. In any case, Toussaint was not won over. When the expedition reached Saint-Domingue in January 1802 it was resisted as an enemy invasion. Leclerc declared Toussaint an outlaw, but the black army held out for five months of fierce and merciless fighting, which devastated afresh much of the colony scarcely yet recovered from a decade of random destruction. Toussaint knew that if he held out long enough, tropical diseases would decimate the French troops as they had the British a few years previously. The process had already begun when restless leading lieutenants began to desert his own dwindling ranks. Eventually a truce was arranged, during which he returned to domestic life. It was a fatal mistake. Within a month the disarmed general was arrested by Leclerc's men. In accordance with the expedition's initial secret instructions he was at once embarked on a ship to France. By then, a consular decree had prohibited any black or mixed-race immigration into France: non-whites of any sort were now deemed too dangerous. Toussaint's pleas for an audience with the first consul were ignored, and he was sent directly to imprisonment in a fortress high in the remote Jura mountains. He only survived there eight months.

With the reopening of the seas, French authority was bolstered in Guadeloupe, and the slave emancipation introduced earlier was initially confirmed. But where slavery had not been abolished, consular policy was to maintain it. This happened in the Indian Ocean islands, and also in Martinique, returned to France under the Peace of Amiens. And on the very day the peace was proclaimed, the slave trade, fundamental for islands where the black population did not renew itself, was re-authorized 'in conformity with the law and regulations existing before ... 1789'. The real problem was how to revive the agricultural prosperity of Caribbean colonies without slavery. Even Toussaint had recognized this difficulty and had begun to introduce a system that still tied ostensibly free and paid 'cultivators' to their plantations. A similar approach was now adopted in Guadeloupe but was rapidly perceived as simply another form of slavery. It provoked an uprising, which was only put down with hundreds of deaths, deportations and even mass suicides among defiant rebels. In the aftermath, slavery was rapidly reintroduced according to previous consular instructions. Only white men were now allowed the status of French citizens. The same regime was also reimposed in Guiana.

News of this soon reached Saint-Domingue from ships carrying deported rebels. The effect was catastrophic. The black generals who had betrayed Toussaint now felt betrayed themselves by a republic that had obviously decided to restore slavery despite repeated assurances. 'All the blacks are persuaded', reported Leclerc in August,

> by letters from France, by the law re-establishing the slave trade, and by the orders . . . re-establishing slavery in Guadeloupe that we wish to enslave them, and I can only manage to disarm them by long and stubborn struggles.

These men do not wish to give up. It must be admitted
that on the eve of finishing everything here, [these] . . .
circumstances have almost destroyed what I have done . . .
Only by force of arms can we any longer put down the
blacks. And then, we need an army and money.[3]

By now, too, disease had seriously begun to decimate the white
troops at his disposal. He had already lost half the men he had
come with, and only ten weeks later, Leclerc himself succumbed
to yellow fever. By then he had reached the conclusion, echoing
the more ferocious generals in the Vendée, that only mass exter-
mination of rebel populations could bring an end to what had
become a widespread popular rebellion.

Now, however, it was something more. Both the leading black
generals, Jean-Jacques Dessalines and Henri Christophe, had
abandoned the allegiance they had forsaken Toussaint for. Notorious
both (in contrast with Toussaint) for their hatred of white col-
onists, they now wanted nothing less than independence. For a
year Leclerc's deputy and successor, Donatien Marie Joseph de
Rochambeau, conducted an increasingly desperate and frenzied
all-out war, with incredible atrocities on both sides. But his forces
continued to shrink, and, with the drift back to war against the
British, no reinforcements from Europe could be spared or safely
transported. Rochambeau finally surrendered to Dessalines' black
army in November 1803. Of the 20,000 seasoned soldiers originally
sent with Leclerc, only 1,200 returned to France, and Rochambeau
himself was captured en route by the British. They were still on the
sea when, in January 1804, Dessalines proclaimed the former colony
as the independent Black Republic of Haiti. It began with systematic massacres of the remaining white population.

By then, Napoleon had given up his dream of recreating a
flourishing transatlantic empire. A final piece in his plan had been
to establish a supply base for the islands on the North American

mainland. To this end he had induced Spain in 1800 to return the vast territory of Louisiana, a former French colony ceded to Spain in 1761. Over the winter of 1802–3 a military expedition was prepared to take possession of New Orleans. As the prospect of renewed naval warfare increased, it never sailed. But the alarming thought of Napoleonic control of the Mississippi delta spurred President Thomas Jefferson into making the first consul an irresistible offer: to buy New Orleans. Napoleon now needed little persuading. With Saint-Domingue virtually lost, the supporting role envisaged for Louisiana was redundant. And the purchase money would help to fund the war which now, in April 1803, seemed inevitable. 'Uncertainties and deliberation are no longer in season,' he told senior ministers, 'I am giving up Louisiana. Not only do I wish to hand over New Orleans, but the whole colony, keeping nothing back. I know the price of what I am giving up ... I am handing it over with deep displeasure. To insist on keeping it would be madness.'[4]

So ended Napoleon's attempt to restore pre-revolutionary colonial glories. Saint-Domingue was lost; so was Louisiana; and the other territories were at the mercy of British seapower until the end of the new war a dozen years later. The disorders unleashed by the Revolution had devastated the economy and society of the colonies, and consular policies, so far from bringing them to an end, had merely prolonged and deepened them. 'The Saint-Domingue affair', he said, looking back from St Helena,

> was very foolish of me ... It was the greatest administrative mistake I ever made. I should have dealt with the black leaders as with the authorities in a province ... left Toussaint Louverture as viceroy, not sent in troops, left everything to the blacks ... In this way the negroes, seeing no white power around them, would have become confident in my system. The colony would have proclaimed slave freedom.

It is true that I would have lost Martinique, for the blacks would have been free, but that would have been done without disorder.[5]

He had hoped to round off the triumphs of 1802 by restoring a stable infrastructure for the flourishing Atlantic economy remembered from before the Revolution. He had thought, as he always did, that overwhelming military force could provide the means. But by the end of the year of European victory, as the decision to sell Louisiana signalled, his colonial hopes had crumbled. As news of accumulating disasters in Saint-Domingue flooded in in January 1803, he exclaimed, 'Damned sugar, damned coffee, damned colonies!'[6] His bid to end revolutionary disorder beyond the seas, in the year of his greatest triumphs since seizing power, had brought about his first significant defeat.

References

Preface

1 Mathieu Molé, *Souvenirs de jeunesse (1793–1803)* (Paris, 1991), p. 327.
2 Jean-Antoine Chaptal, *Mes souvenirs sur Napoléon*, ed. Patrice Gueniffey (Paris, 2009), p. 85.

Introduction

1 Barry E. O'Meara, *Napoleon in Exile; or, A Voice from St Helena*, 5th edn, 2 vols (London, 1822), vol. I, pp. 208–10.
2 Tom Pocock, *A Thirst for Glory: The Life of Admiral Sir Sidney Smith* (London, 1996), pp. 26–33.
3 Ibid., pp. 91–109.
4 Ibid., p. 85.
5 Patrice Gueniffey, *Le Dix-huit brumaire: l'épilogue de la Révolution française* (Paris, 2008), pp. 188–9.
6 Elizabeth Sparrow, *Secret Service: British Agents in France, 1782–1815* (Woodbridge, 1999), p. 189.
7 Maréchal Marmont, *Avec Bonaparte*, ed. Philippe Bulinge (Paris, 2004), p. 359.
8 See the discussions in Sparrow, *Secret Service*, p. 192; Gueniffey, *Le Dix-huit Brumaire*, pp. 171–8.
9 Marmont, *Avec Bonaparte*, p. 359.
10 Sparrow, *Secret Service*, pp. 186–7; Gueniffey, *Le Dix-huit brumaire*, pp. 177–8.
11 Harvey Mitchell, *The Underground War against Revolutionary France: The Missions of William Wickham, 1794–1800* (Oxford, 1965), pp. 188–9; Thierry Lentz, *Le Grand Consulat, 1799–1804* (Paris, 1999), pp. 31–2.
12 '[Ce] bougre-là nous a laissé ici ses culottes pleines de merde,' quoted in A. B. Rodger, *The War of the Second Coalition, 1798 to 1801: A Strategic Commentary* (Oxford, 1964), p. 132.
13 Quoted in Pocock, *Thirst for Glory*, p. 114.

1 Taking Control

1 Général Baron Gourgaud, *Journal de Sainte-Hélène, 1815–1818*, ed. Octave Aubry, 2 vols (Paris, 1944), vol. II, p. 221, 23 August 1817.

2 Général Bertrand, *Cahiers de Sainte-Hélène 1816–1821*, ed. Paul Fleuriot de Langle, 3 vols (Paris, 1949–51), vol. II, p. 428.

3 *Mémoires du comte Miot de Mélito, ancien ministre, ambassadeur, conseiller d'Etat et membre de l'Institut (1788–1815)*, 3 vols (Paris, 1858), vol. I, p. 154.

4 Napoleon Bonaparte, *Correspondance générale*, 15 vols (Paris, 2002–18), vol. I, p. 1081, no. 1822, 26 July 1797.

5 Ibid., pp. 1196–7, no. 2065, to Talleyrand, 21 September 1797.

6 *Mémoires du comte Miot de Mélito*, vol. I, p. 156.

7 *Correspondance générale*, vol. I, p. 1118, no. 1908, to the Directoire exécutif, 16 August 1797.

8 Ibid., vol. II, p. 37, no. 2315, 23 February 1798.

9 Ibid., p. 1042, no. 4655, to Général Dugua, 27 July 1799.

10 Ibid., p. 1089, no. 4762, 10 October 1799.

11 Except the Legislative in 1791, for which, as a former constituent, he was ineligible.

12 Roederer, *Mémoires sur la Révolution, le Consulat et l'Empire*, ed. Octave Aubry (Paris, 1942), pp. 104–5.

13 In the republican calendar 18 Brumaire.

14 John Eldred Howard, *Letters and Documents of Napoleon*, vol. I: *The Rise to Power* (London, 1961), p. 310.

15 Cambacérès, *Mémoires inédits*, vol. I: *La Révolution, le Consulat*, ed. Laurance Chatel de Brancion (Paris, 1999), p. 437.

16 Howard, *Letters and Documents*, vol. I, p. 311.

17 Emmanuel Dieudonné, Comte de Las Cases, *Mémorial de Sainte-Hélène*, vol. I: *28–30 octobre 1815*, ed. Gérard Walter, 2 vols (Paris, 1956), p. 168.

18 Paul Bastid, *Sieyès et sa pensée* (Paris, 1970), p. 255.

19 Isser Woloch, *Napoleon and His Collaborators: The Making of a Dictatorship* (New York, 2001), ch. 5.

20 Roederer, *Mémoires sur la Révolution*, p. 115.

21 Proclamation of 24 Frimaire, Year VIII/15 December 1799.

22 Roederer, *Mémoires sur la Révolution*, p. 120.

23 Proclamation of 4 Nivôse, Year VIII/25 December 1799.

24 Jean-Antoine Chaptal, *Mes souvenirs sur Napoléon*, ed. Patrice Gueniffey (Paris, 2009), p. 85.

25 Quoted in Louis Madelin, *Histoire du Consulat et de l'Empire*, vol. IV:

Le Consulat (Paris, 1939), pp. 28–9.

26 *Correspondance générale*, vol. III, p. 386, no.5639, to the Comte de Provence, 20 Fructidor Year VIII.

2 Winning the War

1 Emmanuel Dieudonné, Comte de Las Cases, *Mémorial de Sainte-Hélène*, vol. I: *28–30 Octobre 1815*, ed. Gérard Walter, 2 vols (Paris, 1956), p. 959.

2 Malcolm Crook, *Toulon in War and Revolution: From the Ancien Régime to the Restoration, 1750–1820* (Manchester, 1991), p. 150.

3 *Diaries and Correspondence of James Harris, First Earl of Malmesbury*, 4 vols (London, 1844), vol. III, p. 420, Malmesbury to Grenville, 25 July 1797.

4 Las Cases, *Mémorial*, vol. I, p. 98.

5 Général Baron Gourgaud, *Journal de Sainte-Hélène, 1815–1818*, ed. Octave Aubry, 2 vols (Paris, 1944), vol. I, p. 115.

6 Napoleon Bonaparte, *Correspondance générale*, 15 vols (Paris, 2002–18), vol. I, p. 1118, no. 1908, 16 August 1797.

7 Ibid., vol. II, p. 38, no. 2315, 23 February 1798.

8 Ibid., p. 1086, no. 4758, to Général Kléber, 22 August 1799; p. 1088, no. 4759, to Poussielgue, 22 August 1799.

9 Speech in the House of Commons, 3 February 1800.

10 *Correspondance générale*, vol. III, p. 310, no. 5455, to Carnot, 20 June 1800.

11 Quoted in Roger Wells, *Insurrection: The British Experience, 1795–1803* (Gloucester, 1986), p. 198.

12 *Correspondance générale*, vol. III, p. 783, no. 6494, draft letter, 17 September 1801.

13 Charles Ross, ed., *Correspondence of Charles, First Marquis Cornwallis*, 3 vols (London, 1859), vol. III, p. 390, Cornwallis to Hawkesbury, 10 November 1801.

14 Ibid., p. 406, Cornwallis to Ross, 7 December 1801.

15 *Diaries and Correspondence of James Harris, First Earl of Malmesbury*, vol. IV, pp. 62–3. The king was referring to the preliminaries rather than the final treaty, but his attitude did not change.

16 Napoléon and Joseph Bonaparte, *Correspondance intégrale, 1784–1818*, ed. Vincent Haegele (Paris, 2007), p. 70, no. 89, Joseph to Napoleon, 6 December 1801.

17 Antoine-Claire Thibaudeau, *Mémoires sur le Consulat, 1799–1804*, ed. François Pascal (Paris, 2013), p. 204.

18 Quoted in André Fugier, *La Révolution française et l'Empire napoléonien* (Paris, 1954), p. 153.

19 Talleyrand, *Mémoires, 1754–1815*, ed. Paul-Louis and Jean-Paul Couchoud (Paris, 1982), pp. 288–9.

20 Thibaudeau, *Mémoires sur le Consulat*, p. 206.

3 Treating with God

1 Henri Gatien Bertrand, *Cahiers de Sainte-Hélène, 1816–1821*, ed. Paul Fleuriot de Langle, 3 vols (Paris, 1949–59), vol. III, pp. 105–6, 27 March 1821.

2 Ibid., vol. I, p. 286, 13 October 1817. But in Emmanuel Dieudonné, Comte de Las Cases, *Mémorial de Sainte-Hélène*, vol. I: *28–30 octobre 1815*, ed. Gérard Walter, 2 vols (Paris, 1956), ch. 8, 17, vol. I, p. 1039, he puts his age at thirteen.

3 Quoted in J. Christopher Herold, *The Mind of Napoleon: A Selection from His Written and Spoken Words* (New York, 1955) p. 107.

4 Quoted in Louis Madelin, *Fouché*, 2 vols (Paris, 1945), vol. I, p. 109.

5 See Patrice Gueniffey, *Bonaparte, 1769–1802* (Paris, 2013), p. 186.

6 Napoleon Bonaparte, *Correspondance générale*, 15 vols (Paris, 2002–18), vol. I, p. 647, no. 1025, Bonaparte to Cacault, 7 Brumaire/28 October 1796.

7 Ibid., p. 802, no. 1315, Bonaparte to Cardinal Mattei, 3 Pluviôse/13 January 1797.

8 Ibid., p. 847, no. 1391, Bonaparte to Executive Directory, 1 Ventôse/19 February 1797.

9 Ibid., p. 1098, no. 1859. Note remise au Ministre du Pape, 16 Thermidor/3 August 1797.

10 Quoted in Gueniffey, *Bonaparte*, p. 544.

11 Decree of 7 Nivôse, Year VIII/28 December 1799, in John Eldred Howard, *Letters and Documents of Napoleon* (London, 1961), p. 331, no. 445.

12 Quoted in Howard, *Letters and Documents*, pp. 367–8, no. 523.

13 Quoted in Thibaudeau, *Mémoires sur le Consulat, 1799–1804*, ed. François Pascal (Paris, 2013), pp. 87–8.

14 'Compte rendu par le citoyen Fourcroy, conseiller d'Etat, de sa mission dans la 12ᵉ division militaire pendant le mois de nivôse An IX', in Félix Rocquain, *L'Etat de la France au 18 brumaire d'après les rapports des conseillers d'Etat chargés d'une enquête sur la situation de la république* (Paris, 1874), p. 134.

15 Roederer, *Mémoires sur la Révolution et l'Empire*, pp. 133–4.

16 Quoted in Rodney J. Dean, *L'Eglise constitutionnelle, Napoléon, et le Concordat de 1801* (Paris, 2004), p. 232.

17 Thibaudeau, *Mémoires sur le Consulat*, p. 93, 'C'est une belle capucinade.'

18 Général Baron Gourgaud, *Journal de Sainte Helène, 1815–1818*, ed. Octave Aubry, 2 vols (Paris, 1944), vol. I, p. 275, 9 January 1817.

19 Bertrand, *Cahiers de Sainte-Hélène*, vol. I, p. 224, 14 May 1817.

20 Quoted in Pierre de la Gorce, *Histoire religieuse de la Révolution française*, 5 vols (Paris, 1912–23), vol. V, p. 324, 30 September 1801. Contrast Stalin's 'How many divisions has the Pope?'

21 Charles François Tristan de Montholon, *Récits de la captivité de l'Empereur Napoléon à Sainte-Hélène*, 2 vols (Paris, 1847), vol. II, pp. 270–71.

22 As reported by Mme de Staël in *Dix années d'exil*, ed. Simone Balayé and Mariella Vianello Bonifacio (Paris, 1996), p. 335.

23 *Correspondance générale*, vol. III, p. 1153, no. 7273, 11 November 1802.

24 For these later quarrels, see Ambrogio A. Caiani, *To Kidnap a Pope: Napoleon and Pius VII* (London, 2021).

4 Restoring Authority

1 Duchesse d'Abrantès, *Souvenirs intimes sur l'enfance, la jeunesse, la vie privée de Napoléon Bonaparte, général et premier consul, 1769–1801* (Paris, 1910), p. 396.

2 Jean-Antoine Chaptal, *Mes souvenirs sur Napoléon*, ed. Patrice Gueniffey (Paris, 2009), p. 135.

3 In *La France libre* – for which he could not find a publisher until the crisis leading to the fall of the Bastille made him famous.

4 Paul de Rémusat, ed., *Mémoires de Madame de Rémusat*, 3 vols (Paris, 1881), vol. I, p. 269 ('gens en veste').

5 Charles François Tristan de Montholon, *Récits de la captivité de l'Empereur Napoléon à Sainte-Hélène*, 2 vols (Paris, 1847), vol. I, p. 340, 26 July 1816.

6 Napoleon Bonaparte, *Correspondance générale*, 15 vols (Paris, 2002–18), vol. I, p. 238, no. 312. To Boinod, commissaire des guerres, 6 Thermidor, Year III/24 July 1795.

7 Alphonse Roserot, ed., *Mémoires de Madame de Chastenay, 1771–1815*, 2 vols (Paris, 1896), vol. I, pp. 281–4.

8 See Malcolm Crook, *Elections in the French Revolution: An Apprenticeship in Democracy, 1789–1799* (Cambridge, 1996), p. 142.

9 *Correspondance générale*, vol. I, p. 1058, no. 1785, 24 Messidor Year V/ 15 July 1797.

10 Ibid., p. 1061, no. 1791, 29 Messidor Year v/17 July 1797.

11 Miot de Melito, *Mémoires du comte Miot de Melito, ancien ministre, ambassadeur, conseiller d'état et membre de l'Institut (1788–1815)*, 3 vols (Paris, 1858), vol. I, p. 156.

12 *Correspondance générale*, vol. I, p. 1081, no. 1822, 8 Thermidor Year v/26 July 1797.

13 Quoted in Louis Madelin, *Histoire du Consulat et de l'Empire*, vol IV: *Le Consulat* (Paris, 1939), pp. 28–9.

14 *Correspondance générale*, vol. II, p. 1119, no. 4823, 7 Nivôse Year VIII/ 28 December 1799.

15 André Michel, ed., *Correspondance inédite de Mallet du Pan avec la Cour de Vienne (1794–1798)*, 2 vols (Paris, 1884), vol. I, pp. 42, 51, 5 January 1795.

16 Paul Bastid, *Sieyès et sa pensée* (Paris, 1970), p. 255.

17 Roederer, *Mémoires sur la Révolution, le Consulat et l'Empire*, ed. Octave Aubry (Paris, 1942), p. 127.

18 *Correspondance générale*, vol. III, pp. 386–7, no. 5639.

19 Cambacérès, *Mémoires inédits*, vol. I: *La Révolution, Le Consulat*, ed. Laurence Chatel de Brancion (Paris, 1999), p. 574.

20 Christophe Pincemaille, ed., *Mémoires de la Reine Hortense* (Paris, 2009), p. 92. He was in fact freely quoting from a character in Voltaire's *Œdipe*, then popular in Paris theatres.

21 Cambacerès, *Mémoires*, vol. I, p. 623.

22 Ibid.

23 Ibid.

24 Thibaudeau, *Mémoires sur le Consulat*, p. 142.

25 Louis Madelin, ed., *Les Mémoires de Fouché* (Paris, 1945), p. 194.

26 Mme de Staël, *Dix années d'exil*, ed. Simone Balayé and Mariella Vianello Bonifacio (Paris, 1996), p. 114.

27 Bertrand, *Cahiers de Sainte-Hélène*, vol. I, p. 59.

28 Quoted in Thierry Lentz, *Le Grand Consulat, 1799–1804* (Paris, 1999), p. 562.

29 Quoted in Henri Gaubert, *Conspirateurs au temps de Napoléon Ier* (Paris, 1962), p. 235.

30 Paul de Rémusat, ed., *Mémoires de Madame de Rémusat*, 3 vols (Paris, 1881), vol. I, p. 390.

5 Curbing Disorder

1 Jean-Antoine Chaptal, *Mes souvenirs sur Napoléon*, ed. Patrice Gueniffey (Paris, 2009), p. 123.

2 Quoted in Marcel Marion, *Le Brigandage pendant la Révolution* (Paris, 1934), p. 35.

3 *Réimpression de l'ancien Moniteur de la réunion des Etats Généraux jusqu'au Consulat*, 32 vols (Paris, 1847), vol. III, pp. 526–7, 4 March 1790.

4 Quoted in Jean-Clément Martin, *Violence et Révolution: essai sur la naissance d'un mythe national* (Paris, 2006), p. 181.

5 Général Baron Gourgaud, *Journal de Sainte-Hélène, 1815–1818*, ed. Octave Aubry, 2 vols (Paris, 1944), vol. I, p. 268, 6 January 1817; Général Bertrand, *Cahiers de Sainte-Hélène 1816–1821*, ed. Paul Fleuriot de Langle, 3 vols (Paris, 1949–51), vol. II, p. 175, 6 January 1817; Charles François Tristan de Montholon, *Récits de la captivité de l'Empereur Napoléon à Sainte-Hélène*, 2 vols (Paris, 1847) vol. II, p. 180, 31 August 1817.

6 Napoleon Bonaparte, *Correspondance générale*, 15 vols (Paris, 2002–18), vol. I, p. 237, no. 311, to Joseph, 30 Messidor Year III/18 July 1795; p. 238, no. 31, to Joseph, 6 Thermidor Year III/24 July 1795.

7 Henry Swinburne, *The Courts of Europe at the Close of the Last Century*, 2 vols (London, 1895), vol. II, p. 105.

8 Ibid., pp. 132–3.

9 Las Cases, *Mémorial*, 16 January 1816.

10 Quoted in Howard G. Brown, *Ending the French Revolution: Violence, Justice and Repression from the Terror to Napoleon* (Charlottesville, VA, 2006), p. 258.

11 *Correspondance générale*, vol. II, p. 1122, no. 4826, to d'Andigné, 9 Nivôse Year VIII/30 December 1800.

12 Ibid., p. 1118, no. 4823.

13 Ibid., p. 1120, no. 4824, to Berthier, 8 Nivôse Year VII/29 December 1799.

14 Ibid., vol. III, p. 39, no. 4872, 24 Nivôse Year VII/14 January 1800.

15 Ibid., p. 102, no.5010, 29 Pluviôse/18 February 1800.

16 Quoted in Marion, *Le Brigandage*, p. 141.

17 Napoléon and Joseph Bonaparte, *Correspondance intégrale, 1784–1818*, ed. Vincent Haegele (Paris, 2007), p. 207, no. 347, 16 May 1806.

18 Letter to Van de Weyer, 29 November 1868, in John Goldworth Alger, *Napoleon's British Visitors and Captives, 1801–1815* (London, 1904), p. 321.

19 'Mémoire de Barbé Marbois, conseiller d'Etat, pour rendre compte de sa mission dans la 13ᵉ division militaire', in Félix Rocquain, *L'Etat de la France au 18 brumaire* (Paris, 1874), pp. 120–21.

20 Quoted in Marion, *Le Brigandage*, p. 207.

21 Quoted in Albert Vandal, *L'Avènement de Bonaparte*, 2 vols (Nelson edn, Paris, no date), vol. II, p. 501.

22 Marquis de Lafayette, *Mémoires, correspondance et manuscrits*, 6 vols (Leipzig, 1837–8), vol. v, p. 184.

23 Chateaubriand, *Mémoires d'outre-tombe*, Book Three, ch. 11.

6 An Experimental Peace

1 A. Aulard, ed., *Paris sous le Consulat: recueil de documents pour l'histoire de l'esprit public à Paris*, 4 vols (Paris, 1906), vol. iii, p. 190.

2 Joyce Hemlow, ed., *The Journals and Letters of Fanny Burney* (Oxford, 1975), vol. v, p. 232. Letter 503, Fanny Burney to her father, 15–19 April 1802.

3 J.A.C. Sykes, ed., *France in Eighteen Hundred and Two described in a series of contemporary letters by Henry Redhead Yorke* (London, 1906), p. 19.

4 Burney, *Journals*, vol. v, p. 232, 18 April 1802.

5 Ibid., p. 239.

6 Johann Friedrich Reichardt, *Un hiver à Paris sous le Consulat*, ed. Thierry Lentz (Paris, 2003) p. 140, 2 December 1802.

7 Francis Blagdon, *Paris as it was and is, or a sketch of the French capital illustrative of the effects of the Revolution*, 2 vols (London, 1803), Letter xxvii, 21 December 1801.

8 Sykes, ed., *France in Eighteen Hundred and Two*, p. 155.

9 J.P.T. Bury and J. C. Barry, eds, *An Englishman in Paris, 1803: The Journal of Bertie Greatheed* (London, 1953), p. 120, 22 April 1803.

10 Reichardt, *Un hiver à Paris*, p. 349, 4 February 1803.

11 Sykes, ed., *France in Eighteen Hundred and Two*, p. 117; Napoleon had brought a bodyguard of moustachioed swordsmen back from Egypt.

12 Duchesse d'Abrantès, *Souvenirs intimes sur l'enfance, la jeunesse, la vie privée de Napoléon Bonaparte, général et premier consul, 1769–1801* (Paris, 1910), p. 373.

13 J. G. Lemaistre, *A Rough Sketch of Modern Paris* (London, 1803), quoted in Constantia Maxwell, *The English Traveller in France, 1689–1815* (London, 1932), p. 241.

14 Quoted in L. G. Mitchell, *Charles James Fox* (Oxford, 1992), p. 174.

15 Aulard, *Paris sous le Consulat*, vol. iii, p. 497. *Moniteur* of 8 August 1802.

16 Jean-Antoine Chaptal, *Mes souvenirs sur Napoléon*, ed. Patrice Gueniffey (Paris, 2009), p. 121.

17 See above, p. 71.

18 Sir John Carr, *The Stranger in France; or, A Tour from Devonshire to Paris* (Baltimore, MD, 1805), p. 37.

19 Oscar Browning, ed., *England and Napoleon in 1803, being the Despatches of Lord Whitworth and Others* (London, 1887), p. 14. Whitworth to Hawkesbury, 20 November 1802.

20 See Epilogue.

21 Browning, *England and Napoleon in 1803*, p. 61, 7 February 1803.

22 Napoleon Bonaparte, *Correspondance générale*, 15 vols (Paris, 2002–18), vol. III, p. 1106, no. 7174, 23 September 1802.

23 Browning, *England and Napoleon in 1803*, p. 82, 21 February 1803.

24 Ibid.; according to Henri Fauville, *La France de Bonaparte vue par les visiteurs anglais* (Aix-en-Provence, 1989), p. 98, citing no other source, the words Napoleon used were *misérables foutaises*.

25 Bury and Barry, eds, *Journal of Bertie Greatheed*, pp. 93–4.

26 Browning, *England and Napoleon in 1803*, p. 137. Whitworth to Hawkesbury, 24 March 1803.

27 *Correspondance générale*, vol. IV, p. 127, no. 7629, 10 May 1803.

28 Ibid., p. 682.

29 Cambacérès, *Mémoires inédits*, vol. I: *La Révolution, Le Consulat*, ed. Laurance Chatel de Brancion (Paris, 1999), p. 677: 'ce penchant pour la dispute, dont il n'a jamais pu se délivrer.'

30 Sykes, ed., *France in Eighteen Hundred and Two*, pp. 240–41.

31 *Mémoires*, vol. I, p. 680.

32 Sykes, ed., *France in Eighteen Hundred and Two*, p. 242.

33 Ibid., p. 231.

34 For Paine's tribulations in America, see John Keane, *Tom Paine: A Political Life* (London, 1995), ch. 12; W. A. Speck, *A Political Biography of Thomas Paine* (London, 2013), ch. 9.

Conclusion

1 On what can reasonably be inferred from these flawed votes, see Malcolm Crook, 'Confidence from Below? Collaboration and Resistance in the Napoleonic Plebiscites', in *Collaboration and Resistance in Napoleonic Europe: State Formation in an Age of Upheaval, c. 1800–1815*, ed. Michael Rowe (Basingstoke, 2003), pp. 19–36.

2 Text in A. Aulard, ed., *Paris sous le Consulat: recueil de documents pour l'histoire de l'esprit public à Paris*, 4 vols (Paris, 1906), vol. III, pp. 134–5.

3 J.P.T. Bury and J. C. Barry, eds, *An Englishman in Paris, 1803: The Journal of Bertie Greatheed* (London, 1953), p. 169.

4 Aulard, ed., *Paris sous le Consulat*, vol. III, p. 130.

5 Quoted in Wolfram Siemann, *Metternich: Strategist and Visionary* (Cambridge, MA, 2019) pp. 220–21.

Epilogue: Cutting Overseas Losses

1 Quoted in Pierre Branda and Thierry Lentz, *Napoléon, l'esclavage et les colonies* (Paris, 2006), p. 49.
2 Roederer, *Mémoires sur la Révolution, le Consulat et l'Empire*, ed. Octave Aubry (Paris, 1942), pp. 131–2.
3 Quoted in Branda and Lentz, *Napoléon, l'esclavage et les colonies*, p. 131.
4 Quoted by Jacques-Olivier Boudon, 'Barbé Marbois et la vente de la Louisiane', in *Portraits croisés de Thomas Jefferson et Napoléon Bonaparte: la cession de la Louisiane*, ed. François Lemaire (Paris, 2005), pp. 72–3.
5 Général Baron Gourgaud, *Journal de Sainte-Hélène, 1815–1818*, ed. Octave Aubry, 2 vols (Paris, 1944), vol. 1, pp. 278–9, 10 January 1817.
6 Roederer, *Mémoires sur la Révolution*, p. 193.

A Note on Sources

Much of the material in this book is based on many years of reading in both primary sources and secondary scholarship on the revolutionary and Napoleonic period. To mention or refer explicitly to a source for every statement or argument would overburden the text with notes of often marginal importance. So the approach has been to give a reference for contemporary quotations, but only occasionally to flag up contentious or unfamiliar points or perspectives from later historiography. There are thousands of books, in many languages, on the French Revolution and on Napoleon. No historian can make use of more than a handful of them. What follows is merely a selection of those I have found most useful.

Printed Primary Sources

All Napoleonic scholarship now begins with the new definitive edition of Napoléon Bonaparte, *Correspondance générale*, now running to fifteen volumes (2004–18). Volumes I–IV have been drawn on here. Fundamental too, although to be used with sceptical caution, are Napoleon's reminiscences recorded during his final exile on St Helena. They are to be found in Barry E. O'Meara, *Napoleon in Exile; or, A Voice from St Helena*, 2 vols (1819); Emmanuel Dieudonné Comte de Las Cases, *Mémorial de Sainte-Hélène* (1823, many subsequent editions of this classic masterpiece, the bible of Bonapartism); Charles François Tristan de Montholon, *Récits de la captivité de l'Empereur Napoléon à Sainte-Hélène*, 2 vols (1847); Gaspard Gourgaud, *Journal de Sainte-Hélène, 1815–1818*, ed. Octave Aubry, 2 vols (1947) and Henri Gatien Bertrand, *Cahiers de Sainte-Hélène, 1816–1821*, ed. Paul Fleuriot de Langle, 3 vols (1949–59).

Another corpus of material is the memoirs of Napoleon's contemporaries. No fewer than 1,527 are listed and appraised in Jean Tulard, *Nouvelle bibliographie critique des mémoires sur l'époque napoléonienne* (Geneva, 1991). Most useful for this study have been those of Cambacérès (*Mémoires inédits*,

2 vols, ed. Laurance Chatel de Brancion, Paris, 1999), Thibaudeau (*Mémoires sur le Consulat, 1799–1804*, ed. François Pascal, 2013), Roederer (*Mémoires sur la Révolution, le Consulat et l'Empire*, ed. Octave Aubry, Paris, 1942), Miot de Mélito (*Mémoires*, 3 vols, Paris, 1873) and Chaptal (*Mes Souvenirs sur Napoléon*, ed. Patrice Gueniffey, Paris, 2009). While memoirs of other leading players, such as Talleyrand (*Mémoires*, ed. P. L. and J. P. Couchoud, 2 vols, 1957), Fouché (*Mémoires*, ed. Louis Madelin, 1945) or Bourrienne (*Mémoires*, 5 vols, ed. Desiré Lacroix, 1899–1900) cannot be ignored, they are all plagued by questions of authenticity or attribution.

Eyewitness accounts of important circumstances and episodes can be found in *Paris sous le Consulat: recueil de documents pour l'histoire de l'esprit public à Paris* (4 vols, ed. Alphonse Aulard, Paris, 1903–4) and the documents in Félix Rocquain, *L'Etat de la France au 18 brumaire* (Paris, 1874). The numerous impressions published by British visitors during the Peace of Amiens are fully listed and assessed in an appendix, pp. 251–67, to Henri Fauville, *La France de Bonaparte vue par les visiteurs anglais* (Aix-en-Provence, 1989). Their presence in France is recorded in John Goldworth Alger, *Napoleon's British Visitors and Captives, 1801–1815* (Westminster, 1904). A German perspective comes from Johann Friedrich Reichardt, *Un hiver à Paris sous le Consulat*, ed. Thierry Lentz (Paris, 2003). The breakdown of the Peace can be followed in *England and Napoleon in 1803, being the Despatches of Lord Whitworth*, ed. Oscar Browning (London, 1887).

Secondary Sources

An indispensable work of reference is the mighty *Dictionnaire Napoléon*, edited by Jean Tulard (2nd edition, Paris, 1989). What Napoleon was doing on any given day can be checked in Louis Garros and Jean Tulard, *Napoléon au jour le jour* (Paris, 2002). Lives of Napoleon are appearing all the time. The most detailed and useful recent ones, covering this period, are Philip Dwyer, *Napoleon: The Path to Power 1769–1799* (London, 2007), Patrice Gueniffey, *Bonaparte 1769–1802* (Paris, 2013) and Michael Broers, *Napoleon, Soldier of Destiny* (London, 2014). An earlier master-piece of 1902, still worth reading though superseded in scholarly detail, is Albert Vandal, *L'Avènement de Bonaparte* (2 vols, undated Nelson edition, Paris and Edinburgh). A more concise recent guide is Malcolm Crook, *Napoleon Comes to Power: Democracy and Dictatorship in Revolutionary France, 1795–1804* (Cardiff, 1998). The men surrounding the first consul, the so-called Brumairians, are introduced by Isser Woloch, *Napoleon and His Collaborators: The Making of a Dictatorship* (New York, 2001). Important general treatments of the period are Thierry Lentz, *Le Grand Consulat,*

1799–1804 (Paris, 1999) and John D. Grainger, *The Amiens Truce: Britain and Bonaparte, 1801–1803* (Woodbridge, 2004).

The origins and course of the revolutionary wars are surveyed in T.C.W. Blanning, *The French Revolutionary Wars, 1787–1802* (London, 1996), and their last phase is covered in detail by A. B. Rodger, *The War of the Second Coalition, 1798–1801: A Strategic Commentary* (Oxford, 1964). Bonapartist versions of the outcome should be considered in the light of sceptical interpretations offered by Paul W. Schroeder, *The Transformation of European Politics, 1763–1848* (Oxford, 1994), and Owen Connelly, *Blundering to Glory: Napoleon's Military Campaigns* (Wilmington, DE, 1987).

A masterly, concise older survey of the religious question is John McManners, *The French Revolution and the Church* (London, 1969). The papal response to France's evolving religious policy is chronicled in Gérard Pelletier, *Rome et la Révolution française: la théologie et la politique du Saint-Siège devant la Révolution française (1789–1799)* (Rome, 2004). A detailed discussion of the negotiation of the concordat may be found in Rodney J. Dean, *L'Eglise constitutionnelle, Napoléon et le concordat de 1801* (Paris, 2004).

The disorderly decade preceding the consulate is reflected on by Jean-Clément Martin, *Violence et Révolution: essai sur la naissance d'un mythe national* (Paris, 2006). The most notorious violent episode, casting its shadow over years to come, is anatomized in David Andress, *The Terror: Civil War in the French Revolution* (London, 2005). Scarcely less traumatic was western resistance to the Revolution, surveyed by Jean-Clément Martin, *La Vendée et la France* (Paris, 1987) and Donald Sutherland, *The Chouans: The Social Origins of Popular Counter-Revolution in Upper Brittany, 1770–1796* (Oxford, 1982) A brief older overview was offered by Marcel Marion, *Le Brigandage pendant la Révolution* (Paris, 1934) but more authoritative is now Howard G. Brown, *Ending the French Revolution: Violence, Justice, and Repression from the Terror to Napoleon* (Charlottesville, VA, 2006).

Revolution in the Caribbean is one of the most rapidly expanding fields. Napoleon's attitudes and policies are fully explored in Pierre Branda and Thierry Lentz, *Napoléon, l'esclavage et les colonies* (Paris, 2006). The revolution in Saint-Domingue is chronicled in Laurent Dubois, *Avengers of the New World: The Story of the Haitian Revolution* (Cambridge, MA, 2004), and its hero's life covered in Sudhir Hazareesingh, *Black Spartacus: The Epic Life of Toussaint Louverture* (London, 2020). Upheavals in the lesser French Antilles are the subject of William S. Cormack, *Patriots, Royalists, and Terrorists in the West Indies: The French Revolution in Martinique and Guadeloupe, 1789–1802* (Toronto, 2019). A broader overview is Alan Forrest, *The Death of the French Atlantic: Trade, War, and Slavery in the Age of Revolution* (Oxford, 2020).

Photo Acknowledgements

The author and publishers wish to express their thanks to the below sources of illustrative material and/or permission to reproduce it. Some locations of artworks are also given below, in the interest of brevity:

Bibliothèque nationale de France, Paris: pp. 7, 38; John Carter Brown Library, Providence, RI: p. 196; The Metropolitan Museum of Art, New York: p. 170; Musée Carnavalet, Histoire de Paris: pp. 16, 74; Musée Cognacq-Jay, Paris: p. 10; Le musée de la Légion d'honneur et des ordres de chevalerie, Paris: p. 114.

Index

Page numbers in *italics* refer to illustrations